What has made Japan's economy stagnant for more than 30 years?
(Original Japanese version title: A system that will make Japan happy)

Preface: Tax system that is unlikely to increase tax revenue

This month again, I could not live on my pension benefits alone. My health is not good, but I am reluctant to go to the hospital due to medical expenses. My savings, which seemed to be sufficient when I retired, are running out. I had hoped that things would get better after the Corona pandemic in 2020, but I was wrong. This is the prospect of retirement for the majority of Japanese people, which will begin in 10 years at the latest.

Nevertheless, we cannot rely on the government for increasing pension benefits or reducing the burden of medical expenses, as Japan's government does not have the money. The reason why the government is somehow still able to get things done is because the Japanese private sector has money where it is. However, this money will dry up in a matter of time if the situation continues. This is because the Japanese government continues to increase its debt, which it has no way of repaying, and the private sector will eventually have no choice but to fill the gap.

How did this happen? It is because Japan's tax revenue has not increased in over 30 years, and the size of the economy effectively peaked more than 20 years ago. The difference between spending and tax revenue from FY1975 to FY2020, the period for which statistics are available, is a total deficit of 1,413.6 trillion yen.

The average tax revenue from FY 2011 to FY 2020 is 53.7 trillion yen per year, while the average expenditure is 107 trillion yen per year. In other words, for the past 10 years, the government has been running an average budget deficit of 53.2 trillion yen per year, equivalent to the total tax revenue.

If this trend continues, Japan's social security system, including medical care, will collapse. Japanese people will be obliged to keep working until they die.

I said "if this trend continues", but there is no need for Japan to continue as it is. There is a solution that could please the Japanese people, the government, as well as our allies who want Japan to be a reliable partner, not a burden. There could be a more likely way to achieve decent economic growth, businesses regaining competitiveness, people's incomes rising, tax revenues increasing, and more money available to fund the social security system and education.

This book analyzes the problems that Japan has been facing for more than 30 years, using charts and tables provided by the government and international organizations and so on, and suggests ways to make almost all parties involved in Japan better off by eliminating the problems. This suggests that almost no one can be happy in the current Japanese system. It is up to you, just like buying or selling in the market, to decide whether you would endure and wait for the collapse or change the status quo and choose to be happy.

Do you the readers know that you can find this chart on the Ministry of Finance's website titled "Fiscal Considerations for the Future of Japan"?

Chart 00: Trends in Japan's fiscal balance (Source: Ministry of Finance)

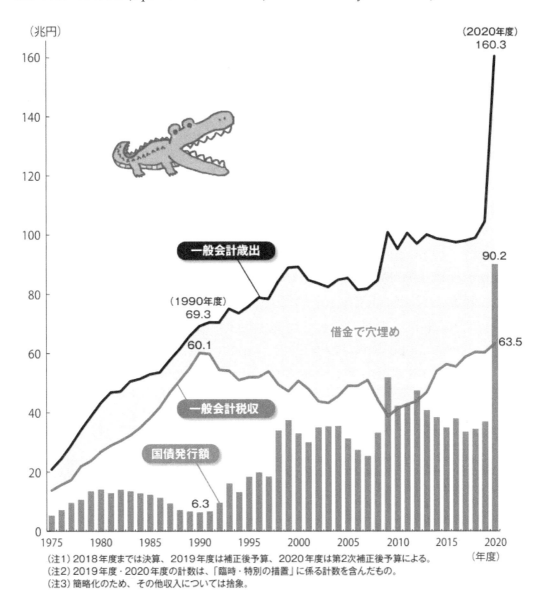

(Note: All other charts and tables are translated into English)

Chart 00 shows Japan's budget balance from FY 1975 to FY 2020. The upper line shows the trend of expenditure. The lower line shows tax revenue. The shadow area sandwiched between the two lines is the budget deficit. The bottom bars show the amount of new government bonds issued to finance the deficit, which basically corresponds to the shadow area.

This picture of a crocodile with its mouth wide open has appeared on the page for at least several years, symbolizing Japan's budget deficit that has only expanded but cannot be closed. But with the expansion of spending on the far right of the chart, the upper jaw of the crocodile has come off. In other words, while the tax revenue for FY 2020 is estimated to be just a bit over 60 trillion yen, the expenditure has exceeded 160 trillion yen. If you look closely, you can see tears in the crocodile's dull eyes.

Yet the 63.5 trillion yen in tax revenue has been revised downward to 60.8 trillion yen due to the Corona pandemic and the halt in economic activity to deal with it, while spending has been increased to 175.7 trillion yen in the third supplementary budget to get the halted economy back on its feet. This indicates that the fiscal deficit for FY 2020 will be over 110 trillion yen. In fact, new government bond issuance, which was estimated to be 90.2 trillion yen, is now expected to be over 112 trillion yen. Since this is supposed to fill the deficit, the deficit is almost twice as large as the tax revenue.

(Note: These figures have been revised several times and may be revised in the future, but minor revisions are not important to the big picture and can be ignored as they are within the margin of error.)

Chart 00#: Trends in Japan's fiscal balance (Source: Ministry of Finance; with figures are added to Chart 00 and resized)

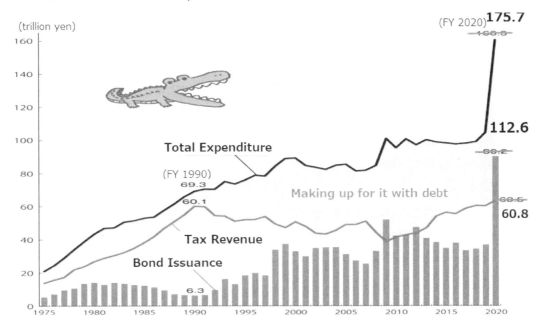

(Note: translated by Arata Yaguchi)

The creators of the chart 00 at the Ministry of Finance seem to have a similar view to mine, because they dare to emphasize the tax revenue of 60.1 trillion yen for FY 1990. Also, the severity of the deficit appears to be more pronounced in the vertically longer chart than the resized chart 00#. What this tells us is that Japan's tax revenue has not increased for 30 years. On the other hand, as spending has generally continued to increase during the period, therefore the deficit has been growing and the government debt has been accumulating.

I see the reason for this as the consumption tax introduced in FY 1989, which has led to a decline in tax revenues, and the accumulation of budget deficits and public debt, which has put Japan's social security system in jeopardy. I think that all Japanese voters should see these charts, and I would like to think that at least politicians who talk about raising the consumption tax should have seen them.

I think it is up to you the readers to decide for yourselves whether you think that is why we have no choice but to raise the consumption tax further, or whether, like me, you see this problem as a result of the introduction of the consumption tax. In other words, how can Japan's social security system be maintained without all Japanese people seriously considering the implications of a budget deficit of more than 110 trillion yen in a single fiscal year, which is twice as much as tax revenue?

What's wrong with the consumption tax? Government budget is financed by the taxes on the people's activity. The government builds infrastructure, creates an environment where business can be conducted safely, and collects taxes on the share of wealth created by the people through production. At this time, income tax and corporate tax are collected according to the results of production.

The consumption tax, on the other hand, is like an entry fee charging 10% on seeds and seedlings for the production, instead of waiting for the harvest in the fall. This will cause production to stagnate because some of the source of the harvest has been taken away, which in turn will reduce tax revenue.

The tax system is the foundation of a country. It is useless to fix leaks and windbreaks through administrative reform when the foundation is rotten. Therefore, I tried to use many charts and tables so that the readers can understand what is going on just by looking at the charts. Unless more people do understand the consumption tax, Japan will not improve.

As a former money manager, I have been familiar with charts and tables for 40 years. I am good at reading and understanding charts. It would be my pleasure if I could help you the readers to understand these charts one by one.

Mr. Shinzo Abe, the former prime minister, was in office for 2,822 consecutive days and a total of 3,188 days when combined with his first term, both of which are the longest in history. This means that if the Japanese economy has been lackluster for the past couple of decades, he is the most responsible for it in history. Nevertheless, the economic recovery period under Abenomics lasted 71 months, just two months shy of the 73 months of the "Izanami boom" (February 2002 to February 2008), which was considered the longest postwar expansion.

However, both the Izanami boom and Abenomics just took time to recover slowly from their depressions, and did not leave behind anything to be proud of. On the contrary, they have left behind a number of big problems for Japan in the future.

The succeeding prime ministers have inherited such issues from their legendary predecessor. Let's take a look at some of the issues that came to mind.

1. Huge accumulated budget deficit
2. Huge outstanding public debt
3. A tax system that cannot expect to increase tax revenues
4. A social security system that will virtually collapse if the current situation continues
5. Challenge the declining birthrate and aging population
6. Monetary policy in a state of near-limitless easing (the remaining policies are neutral or tightening)
7. Disappearance of short-term interest rate products
8. The government bond market has lost its function
9. BOJ stock holdings exceed well over 30 trillion yen
10. Economic downturn ruined by hollowing out of industries, reliance on inbound tourism, the consumption tax hike, and countermeasures against Corona pandemic
11. Era of closing rush of business
12. The widening gap between the rich and the poor
13. Diplomacy in anticipation of a full-scale confrontation between the U.S. and China

14. Life with Covid-19 and future measures against other epidemics
15. Countermeasures against global warming, which has begun to rage

Each of these issues is so big that it's rather hard to stop talking about them. I can understand why Mr. Abe, who had been confronting these issues, thought of resigning on the day he broke the record for consecutive terms in office. How could he possibly improve the problems that he himself had worsened over 2,822 days, or 3,188 days if we include his first term, in the short remainder of his term?

The main theme of this book is that the consumption tax hike, which is supposed to be the source of funding for social security expenses, has instead increased social security expenses through the economic downturn caused by the tax hike. At the same time, it has reduced total tax revenue, which is the source of funding. This is the main cause of the huge accumulated budget deficit and the huge public debt, which threatens the existence of the social security system.

I also see that through the economic downturn, it has weakened the competitiveness of companies, worsened the working environment, and led to a widening gap between the rich and the poor.

It also points out that in order to stimulate the deteriorating economy, BOJ has introduced negative interest rate policy which has extremely harmful side effects, made over-issuance of currency and fiscal financing that will ruin the country's credibility in the future, and stock ownership of private companies by the central bank. Thus, Japan's monetary policy has lost its function eventually.

After analyzing these charts and tables, I have come to the conclusion that a country can prosper or perish depending on its tax system. Since FY 1989, Japan has had a tax system that cannot increase tax revenue. Based on the chart data, I will explain how this has created most of the 15 issues listed above.

This strongly suggests that Japan can return to decent economic growth if only the tax system is restored to what it was during the high growth and bubble periods. Specifically, the consumption tax should be abolished, the progressive income tax rate should be increased, and the corporate tax rate should be raised. Without a return to a tax system that generates more tax revenue, Japan's social security system will collapse.

The maintenance of the social security system is everyone's matter. Everyone is supposed to be a recipient of a pension in the future. Everyone is using the health insurance system. No one can say for sure that he or she will not be covered by unemployment insurance. Even if you never rely on such benefits, you are paying social insurance premiums at the moment, and if things continue as they are now, your burden of insurance premiums will inevitably rise. The day is coming when the private sector will be forced to fill the government's massive debt.

I hope this book will help you the readers to understand the Japanese system.

Table of Contents

Preface: Tax system that is unlikely to increase tax revenue   ...1

Chapter 1: The Tax System That Destroyed Japan ... 17
1. Tax revenue not increasing even if tax rates are raised ... 17
2. Consumption tax revenue has traded off with growth rate, income tax revenue, and corporate tax revenue ... 21
3. Consumption tax has stopped economic growth ... 25
4. Growth rate from Abenomics was almost zero ... 30
5. Contribution of the Izanami boom was negative in terms of tax revenue ... 32
6. The miracle of the world economy has changed from Japan to China ... 35
7. What is the real contribution of Abenomics? ... 42
8. Transformation of employment condition ... 45
9. Japan's real wages are diverging from the rest of the world ... 48
10. Turning point for nominal wages also coincides with consumption tax hike ... 51
11. Money supply has increased 11.2 times since 1997 ... 53
12. The Bank of Japan "only sees prices" ... 56
13. The gap between banks' deposits and loans is 290 trillion yen ... 60
14. Introduction of negative interest rate policy ... 65
15. Abenomics has destroyed the interest rate market ... 68
16. Income transfer from the private sector to the government ... 72
17. Price trends ... 75
18. Consumption tax hikes have led to disinflation ... 77
19. Consumption tax cannot cover social security costs ... 79
20. Debt-dependent finances ... 82
21. The introduction of the consumption tax was combined with the reduction in the corporate tax rate ... 85
22. Gains from lowering the corporate tax rate ... 88
23. Number of companies with deficits also increased rapidly ... 91
24. Consumption tax is deducted from sales ... 94

25. Income tax ... 98
26. Individual resident tax ... 101
27. Lies and truths of "One For All, All For One" ... 105
28. Downgrade ... 108
29. Ballooning public debt ... 113
30. Greece and Italy have had austerity measures ... 116
31. Japan is ranked 113th out of 113 countries ... 118
32. How about in terms of net debt outstanding? ... 120

Chapter 2: The Widening Wealth Gap Created ... 124
33. The widening gap between the rich and the poor created ... 124
34. The widening wealth gap can be stopped! ... 129
35. Tax revenue trend of Japan ... 132
36. Tax revenue structure of Japan ... 134
37. Tax revenue trend of Denmark ... 136
38. Tax revenue structure of Denmark ... 141
39. Tax revenue trend of Sweden ... 145
40. Tax revenue structure of Sweden ... 149
41. Government spending in 32 OECD countries ... 151
42. Trends in the fiscal balance of Japan, Denmark and Sweden ... 153
43. Trends in income tax rates in major economies ... 156
44. Global trends in corporate tax rates ... 158
45. Only a handful of countries have budget surpluses ... 160
46. Value of currency ... 166

Chapter 3: The Social Security System on the Eve of Collapse ... 171
47. Japan's public social security expenditures ... 171
48. Breakdown of social security expenditures and source of funds ... 174
49. Dependence of the elderly on pensions ... 176
50. National health insurance ... 178
51. Medical expense per capita ... 180
52. Government spending on education ... 183
53. Trends in social security-related expenditures ... 186

54. Trends in burden rate of the people ... 189
55. Pyramid that became a diamond ... 191
56. Causes of death among Japanese ... 194
57. Estimate of Ministry of Health, Labour and Welfare ... 196

Afterword: From decline to prosperity ... 199

References ... 204
About the author: Arata Yaguchi ... 208

Reference: Original Japanese Version

https://www.amazon.co.jp/dp/B092W1M8MZ/

日本が幸せになれるシステム: グラフで学ぶ、年金・医療制度の守り方 Kindle版

矢口 新 ・(著)　形式: Kindle版

8個の評価

すべての形式と版を表示

Kindle版（電子書籍）
¥ 0 kindle unlimited
Kindle Unlimited 会員は、このタイトルを追加料金なし（¥0）で読み放題
¥800 Kindle 価格
獲得ポイント: 8pt

ペーパーバック
¥ 1,980
獲得ポイント: 20pt
¥1,980 より 1 新品

著者をフォロー

矢口 新　＋ フォロー

みなさんは日本政府のコロナ対策が行き当たりばったりたとは思われないだろうか？ 緊急事態宣言で日常生活の継続に急ブレーキをかけたかと思えば、Go To などで急いで加速させ、再度感染者が増えれば、急ブレーキをかけているからだ。また、通常の日常生活に戻るにはワクチンが必要だと言いながら、日本では自前のワクチンすらない。

その大きな要因の1つには日本政府にはカネがないことだ。予算が限られているために打つ手打つ手が中途半端になる。それでも政府は民間のカネを当てにし、返済の当てのない借金を増やしつづけているが、いずれは民間の資金でも穴埋めできなくなる。このままでは、年金や医療を含めた日本の社会保障制度は崩壊する。日本人は死ぬまで働きつづけることを義務づけられる。日本政府は過去に預金封鎖し、国民の資産を没収した前歴を持っているのだ。

どうしてこうなったのか？ それは日本の税収が30年以上も増えておらず、経済規模の事実上のピークも20数年前だからだ。こんな国は世界を見渡してもほとんどない。

1988年度の税収は50.8兆円で、税収に消費税が加わった1989年度から2019年度までの31年

What has made Japan's economy stagnant for more than 30 years?

Original Japanese version title:
A system that will make Japan happy

How to protect the pension and medical care systems

ARATA YAGUCHI

To my Children

For my Grandchildren

Chapter 1: The Tax System That Destroyed Japan

1. Tax revenue not increasing even if tax rates are raised

Chart 01: Consumption tax and total tax revenue (Source: Ministry of Finance with arrows consumption tax rates inserted)

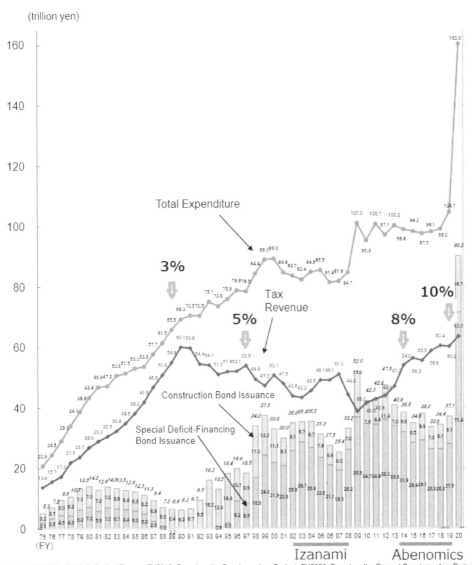

(Note1) FY1975 - FY2018: Settled Figures. FY2019: Based on the Supplementary Budget. FY2020: Based on the Second Supplementary Budget
(Note2) Following bonds are excluded: Ad-hoc Special Deficit-Financing Bonds issued in FY1990 as a source of funds to support peace and reconstruction activities in the Persian Gulf Region. Tax reduction-related Special Deficit-Financing Bonds issued in FY1994 - FY1996 to make up for decline in tax revenue due to a series of income tax cuts preceding consumption tax hike from 3% to 5%. Reconstruction Bonds issued in FY2011 as a source of funds to implement measures for the Reconstruction from the Great East Japan Earthquake and Pension-related Special Deficit-Financing Bonds issued in FY2012 and FY2013 as a source of funds to achieve the targeted national contribution to one-half of basic pension.
(Note3) FY2019 and FY2020 : Including Temporary and Special Measures

Chart 01 is from the "About Japan's Finances" section of the Ministry of Finance's website, with the consumption tax rate and the long-term economic recovery period written in. The upper line shows the change in expenditure (government spending) from FY 1975 to FY 2020, the lower line shows the change in tax revenue, and the bars below show the amount of public debt (government bonds) issued for the fiscal year. The term "special " means that deficits are considered special cases because of the need for fiscal balance.

Do you the readers know when Japan's tax revenue peaked? For the record, it was 60.4 trillion yen in FY 2018. And then in FY 2020 (after downward + upward revisions) it was set at 60.8 trillion yen.

This is the result of Abenomics, but it was achieved through a combination of measures that would have been considered forbidden in the past, such as negative interest rate policy, money supply that exceeds the size of the economy, fiscal financing (The central bank, which is capable of producing currency, buys government bonds, effectively allowing the government to produce its own currency and eliminating the need for fiscal discipline. In Japan, this is against the law.), and central bank ownership of private companies. As we will see later, they were unsustainable and left an excessive burden on the next generation. Nevertheless, the effects were only temporary.

Before that, tax revenue peaked at 60.1 trillion yen in FY 1990, and it took a whopping 28 years to break the record high, and even then, it only returned to almost the original level. During that period, tax revenues sometimes dropped to 38.7 trillion yen at one point.

Chart 01, which shows tax revenue as lower line, showing 60.2 trillion yen for FY 2019 and 63.5 trillion yen for FY 2020, but tax revenue for FY 2019 has already been announced as being 58.4 trillion yen, and for FY 2020 the figure was once revised downward to 55.1 trillion yen, and then to 60.8 trillion yen.

On the other hand, the expenditure shown by the upper line is expected to be

175.7 trillion yen in FY 2020, and the amount of new government bonds issued to finance the deficit is said to be over 112 trillion yen. In other words, anyone can see that the situation of Japan's finances is critical.

This surge in spending was used for counter-Corona measures, including the uniform 100,000 yen payment to each individual, Go-To campaign, and Abe's masks. Rather than spending for positive economic development, these expenditures are more likely to be used to make up for the loss of halted economic activity, and are not likely to lead to increased tax revenue in the future. In other words, there is no prospect of closing the deficit of over 110 trillion yen.

Initially, the Japanese government decided to take short-term measures to deal with the Corona, so it did not pay much attention to minimizing the damage to the national economy. Since the government's policies caused losses to the people, these expenditures were unavoidable in order to protect the livelihood of the people. Nevertheless, from the perspective of national management, including the maintenance of a social security system that protects the people's health not only from the current Corona pandemic but also in the long term, the fact that the government halted economic activities in this way is itself a problem.

The bigger problem, however, is that tax revenues have not increased even with the Izanami boom and Abenomics. This is basically the same for Japan's public finances over the past 30 years, meaning that the country has been running up deficits because it has been unable to get by on its limited tax revenues. The bar chart at the bottom of Chart 01 shows the amount of government bonds issued, which is the amount of money newly borrowed by the government in a given year. It is generally the same amount as the deficit for a single year, which is sandwiched between two lines.

Please look at the lower line in Chart 01. Since the introduction of the consumption tax, the tax rate has been raised three times, but tax revenue has not increased at all, and even appears to be decreasing. This means that the prospect of a future consumption tax hike leading to an increase in tax revenue is slim, and in fact it is more likely to lead to a decrease in tax revenue.

The breakdown of expenditures will be discussed later, but as can be seen from the trends up to FY 1990 in Chart 01, even if the expenditures shown by the upper line increase, if the tax revenues shown by the lower line follow and increase, the gap will not widen and the budget deficit can be considered to be under control. After FY 1990, however, tax revenues began to decline, despite the growth in spending, and despite the introduction of the consumption tax in FY 1989.

The decline in total tax revenue has been repeated since FY 1997, when the consumption tax rate was raised to 5%. This makes it more reasonable to think that the tax revenue decreased because of the consumption tax hike, rather than that it decreased in spite of it.

Do Japanese politicians still think that the consumption tax hike is necessary to secure financial resources for social security? Don't they think it's strange to think that the consumption tax hike will be a source of revenue for social security when there is a high probability that tax revenue will decrease?

2. Consumption tax revenue has traded off with growth rate, income tax revenue, and corporate tax revenue

Chart 02: Tax revenue and nominal GDP growth (Source: Compiled from data of the Ministry of Finance and the Cabinet Office)

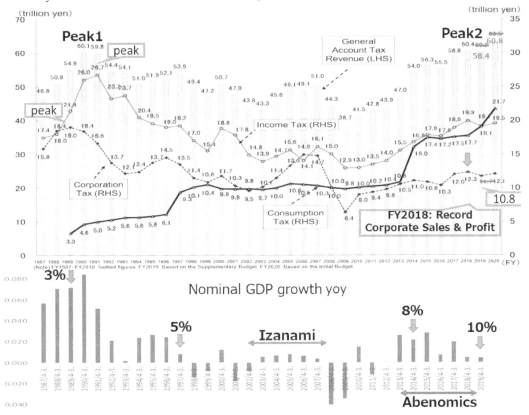

From the upper part of Chart 02, we can see the trends in Japan's total tax revenue since FY 1987 (bars), income tax revenue (thin solid line), corporate tax revenue (dotted line), and consumption tax revenue (thick solid line). The lower part shows the change in nominal GDP (gross domestic product) over the same period compared to the previous year. The arrows indicate when the consumption tax was introduced and the tax rate. In addition, the period of long-term economic expansion is indicated.

Although we have introduced the consumption tax and have continued to raise the tax rate, we see a decline in tax revenue. Why is that? We may find the answer by looking at the breakdown of tax revenue and the economic growth rate in Chart 02.

In the same year that the consumption tax was introduced, corporate tax revenue, shown by the dotted line in Chart 02, peaked and has since declined to nearly half of it. Two years after the introduction of the consumption tax, income tax revenue, shown by the thin solid line, peaked and is now less than two-thirds of what it was. Because of the sharp decline in income tax revenue, the total tax revenue shown in the bar chart peaked one year after the introduction of the consumption tax, despite the new revenue source of the consumption tax shown in the thick solid line.

The bars in the bottom graph of Chart 02 show the growth of nominal GDP (the size of the economy) over the previous year. The momentum of the bubble economy is sustained for a while after the introduction of the consumption tax, but it clearly begins to slow down after FY 1990. This is the period when the bubble economy burst, but since tax hikes are also a means of curbing economic overheating, the additional tightening effect of the introduction of the consumption tax can be seen as having successfully killed the economy.

And from FY 1997, when the consumption tax rate was raised to 5%, the Japanese economy experienced negative growth. The Asian currency crisis occurred during this period. Anyhow for some reason, Japan was the only country that remained stagnant even after the other countries in the region had recovered from the crisis. Rather, Japan's economy was in a state of internal and external distress due to the tax hike and the Asian currency crisis.

Considering that many financial institutions such as the Nippon Credit Bank, Hokkaido Takushoku Bank, and Yamaichi Securities went bankrupt that year, and that the number of suicides skyrocketed after that, it is clear that the consumption tax rate hike at that time was an impossible policy for the government. The "Izanami economy," which has been called the longest postwar expansion, was a slow recovery from the worst period of the post-war Japanese economy. I don't see the point of boasting only about the long period of economic expansion, as seen in the chart.

Abenomics did indeed lead to economic growth up to a certain point, but as mentioned above, it left many problems for future generations because of the many "forbidden measures" it took. It will be explained later that even the growth that was obtained through such efforts has vanished after all.

The consumption tax revenue is shown as a thick solid line. The consumption tax is touted as a "stable source of revenue. As can be seen in Chart 02, it has indeed been a stable source of tax revenue since its introduction and has now become the largest source of revenue for the Japanese government.

Nevertheless, the meaning of a stable source of revenue indicates that the government has been a major burden on households and businesses by steadily deducting money from them even as the economy shrank. And it also implies that this has prolonged deflation.

A stable source of revenue also means that tax revenues are stable even during periods of economic expansion. Even when the economy expands, tax revenue does not increase that much, and only when the tax rate is raised does the consumption tax revenue increase noticeably, as seen in Chart 02.

What this Chart 02 clearly shows is that Japan's total tax revenue has declined because income tax revenue and corporate tax revenue have declined in exchange for the consumption tax revenue. The most significant reason for the decline in tax revenue is that the consumption tax leads to economic recession. In other words, the consumption tax has a trade-off relationship with the rate of economic growth.

Another factor in the decline in tax revenue is the reduction in the corporate and income tax rates, which will be discussed later. In fact, at the height of the

Abenomics effect in FY 2018, corporate sales and corporate profits were both the largest on record, but corporate tax revenue was 12.3 trillion yen, only 65% of the FY 1989 level, due to the reduction in the corporate tax rate.

Although we have introduced the consumption tax and have continued to raise the tax rate, we see a decline in tax revenue. Why is that? This is because the consumption tax has a trade-off relationship with the rate of economic growth, so every time the tax rate is raised, the economy gets worse. Therefore, tax revenues that are highly correlated with the economy and profits, such as income tax revenues and corporate tax revenues, will decline. In addition, this is because the tax rates for income tax and corporate tax, which were the most significant sources of revenue, have been reduced.

The consumption tax hike will reduce total tax revenue. Despite this, it is fair to say that the idea that the consumption tax hike will be a source of revenue for social security is an extremely irrational one, contrary to the data, isn't it?

3. Consumption tax has stopped economic growth

Chart 03: Trends in nominal GDP and personal consumption and consumption tax rate (Source: Compiled from data of the Cabinet Office)

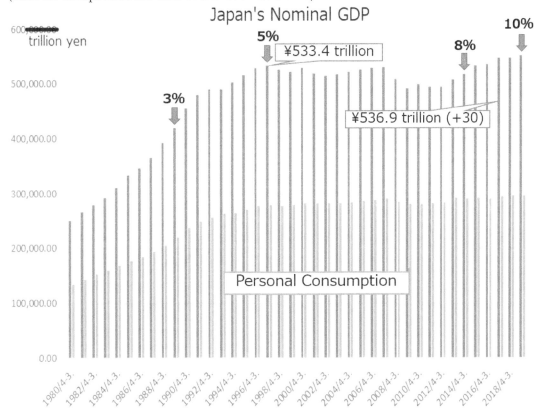

In Chart 03, the longer bars show the trend in nominal Japan's GDP (Gross Domestic Product) from FY 1980 to FY 2019. The shorter bars are personal consumption, the largest component of Japan's GDP. We see Japan's nominal GDP in yen, because the GDP in US dollars is affected by the exchange rate, although it is easier to compare Japan with other countries, as in the data from the United Nations Statistics Division described below. And the real GDP is affected by the inflation rate.

This shows that even during periods of economic contraction, personal consumption has been stable, and taxing it here would provide a stable source of revenue. On the other hand, the fact that the government has uniformly imposed taxes even during periods of economic slowdown suggests that it has become a burden on households and business activity. The possibility that this has prolonged the economic slowdown has already been discussed above.

Japan's nominal GDP began to slow down in FY 1990, the year after the consumption tax was introduced, and began to decline in FY 1997, the year the tax rate was raised to 5%. And the economic scale of 533.4 trillion yen in FY 1997 became the peak for the next 19 years. It was topped in FY 2016, when the calculation method was revised and added 30 trillion yen to the figure, bringing the total to 536.9 trillion yen.

GDP and other figures in the national accounts are compiled based on various basic statistics such as "the Input-Output table". Of these basic statistics, key statistics such as "the Input-Output table" and "the national census" are published about once every five years, and the national accounts are revised significantly (standard revision) about once every five years in accordance with these statistics. As a result, the figure for FY 2016 was 536.9 trillion yen, and about 507 trillion yen if it should have been under the old calculation, topping the previous record. However, this figure is not very encouraging when compared to overseas figures.

According to data from the United Nations Statistics Division, Japan's nominal GDP in 1989, the year the consumption tax was introduced, was $3.054 trillion in terms of today's US dollars. Since the world economy at that time was worth $20.686 trillion, this means that Japan's share of the world economy was 14.8%. (See: Table 01 below.)

The most recent figure in the same document, the size of Japan's economy in 2019, is $5.0825 trillion. Japan has grown 1.66 times in 30 years. Meanwhile, the world's nominal GDP has grown 4.23 times to $87.445 trillion. As a result, Japan's share of the world economy has dropped to 5.8%.

The Japanese economy was even called a miracle when it grew fast from the rubble after World War II to one-seventh of the world economy. At the time, the strength of the economy was considered to come from the nature of the Japanese people and the culture of their companies. However, after around 1989, the Japanese economy rapidly deteriorated and was left behind by the world's economic growth. This in turn became a mystery to the world economy. And the cause of the stagnation came to be blamed on the nature of the Japanese people and the culture of their companies. The evaluation of the Japanese people suddenly took a 180-degree turn.

This suggests that economists around the world have relied on vague things like nature and culture to explain the collapse of the Japanese economy, rather than looking for a solid structure. This is a common occurrence. For example, John Maynard Keynes, one of the foremost economists, still continues to mislead investors by explaining that "stock investing is like a beauty contest" in terms of mind rather than structural factors. He said in Chapter 12 of his work, The General Theory of Employment, Interest and Money (1936), to explain price fluctuations in equity markets. It describes a beauty contest where judges are rewarded for selecting the most popular faces among all judges, rather than those they may personally find the most attractive.

In the actual stock market, there are not only participants who are "motivated" to vote for a stock because they think it is attractive, but there are also participants who buy and sell because of "conditions". When they sell stocks for cash because of their financial situation, they sell even if they think they are attractive. In the case of policy buying, appearance is not an issue.

An example of this in the current Japanese stock market is the Bank of Japan's purchases of stock ETFs through its quantitative easing policy. As of the end of September 2020, the Bank of Japan's holdings of stocks amounted to 34.6 trillion yen in terms of purchase value, contributing greatly to the underpinning of Japanese stocks. The Bank of Japan buys stock ETFs based on market capitalization, liquidity, etc. People who think that investing in stocks is like a beauty contest cannot understand such stock prices.

I call this theory the Tapestry Price Action Theory and explain it in detail in my books on investment. If you are interested in it, please search for "Practical, Surviving Dealing" or "Arata Yaguchi's Short-Term Trading Class". I'm not going to go into it here because it's not the subject of this book, but what a romantic group of people economists are!

Japanese corporate executives were generally the same way, and the dominant argument was that the reason things went wrong after 1990 was because their own methods were not good enough. Later, Japan was urged to learn from the U.S. under the banner of globalization. However, the more we learned and the more we accepted the advice, the more we lost the good qualities of Japan that had once made Japan, in part, the best in the world. Then, we began to find out the parts of ourselves that still couldn't change, and reflected on ourselves that that was why we were no good.

At the beginning of his tenure, Bank of Japan Governor Haruhiko Kuroda said that "appealing to the mindset" of the Japanese people would have the greatest effect in overcoming deflation. This is the same kind of psychological approach as saying that the economy is "spirit". If that is the case, then the Japanese people were full of energy until around 1989, when they suddenly became weak, and this has continued for more than 30 years.

In the 1980s, when I was working as a foreign exchange and bond dealer for financial institutions, there were some senior people who believed that the market was a sentiment. However, in reality, if you bought big, the market would go up, and if you held on to it for a long time, the short sellers would not be able to resist buying back, and the market went up. The market did not go up because of the bullishness, but because of the large amount of money and the Staying Power. Later, the people who were talking about sentiment disappeared when the bubble burst. This strongly suggests that the biggest reason for the stock market rally at the end of 2020 is that the Bank of Japan continues to buy and hold large amounts of stocks and that short sellers are buying back stocks.

I don't think we hear the phrase "appeal to the mindset" from Bank of Japan Governor Kuroda anymore. Nevertheless, despite the unprecedented power play by BOJ, including the massive supply of funds, negative interest rate policy, and stock purchases, the economy has yet to break out of deflation. I see the reason for this as the "most effective" tightening of fiscal policy. The introduction of the consumption tax and the increase in the tax rate did more than anything else to stall the Japanese economy.

4. Growth rate from Abenomics was almost zero

Chart 04: Trends in nominal GDP and growth rate and consumption tax rate (Source: Compiled from data of the Cabinet Office)

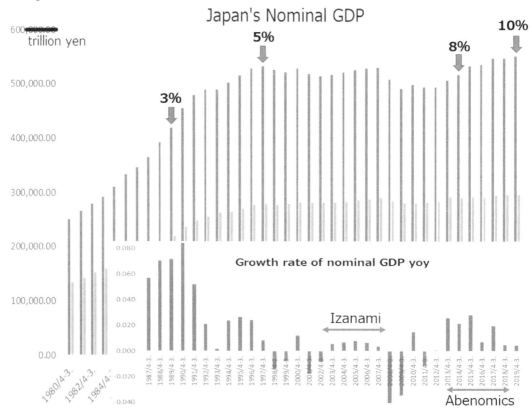

The bars in the lower part of Chart 04 are showing the year-on-year growth rate of nominal GDP since FY 1987 overlaid on the nominal GDP trends from FY 1980 to FY 2019 seen in the previous Chart 03. In Chart 03, the negative growth since FY 1997, when the consumption tax rate was raised to 5%, can be clearly seen, but the economic slowdown since FY 1990 may not be felt, so the growth rate compared to the previous year was inserted as an overlay.

Although the consumption tax was introduced in FY 1989, the bubble economy continued to gain momentum. But after FY 1990, although the size of the economy itself continued to expand, as shown in the long bars, the growth rate slowed down, as shown in the short bars.

Then, after the consumption tax rate was raised to 5% in FY 1997, the economy experienced negative growth for four out of five years. After that, Japan's economy temporarily recovered to 530.9 trillion yen with the Izanami boom, but shrank to 492 trillion yen with the Lehman shock. And it will have to wait for Abenomics to recover 500 trillion yen.

In addition to the aforementioned series of forbidden measures, Abenomics will finally break the FY 1997 peak in FY 2016 by revising the calculation method. Still, economic growth slowed when the consumption tax rate was raised to 8% in FY 2014.

However, even though the economy has reached the peak, the weakness of the Japanese economy after the hollowing out of the manufacturing industry advanced by globalization and in turn relying on inbound tourism, finally resulted in negative growth when consumer spending fell due to the increase in the consumption tax rate to 10% in October 2019.

This was followed by a halt in economic activity due to the counter-Corona measures, which resulted in a return to an annualized 506.6 trillion yen in the April-June 2020 period. In other words, from a macroeconomic point of view, the growth rate of Abenomics, which attempted to preempt future growth with a series of forbidden measures, resulted in almost zero growth, leaving only the paying bill to the next generation.

5. Contribution of the Izanami boom was negative in terms of tax revenue

Chart 05: Expenditure, tax revenue, JGB issuance, JGB outstanding and major economic events (Source: Ministry of Finance website)

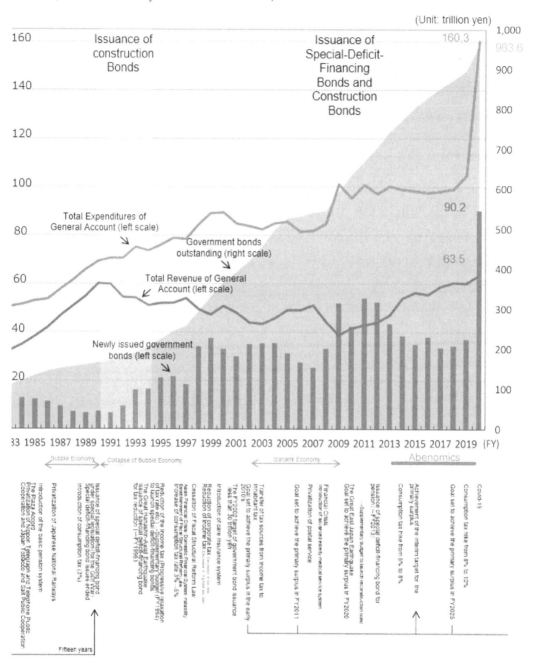

Chart 05 is from the Ministry of Finance's website, with only the Abenomics period inserted. This figure shows the trends in expenditure (upper line: left scale), tax revenue (lower line: left scale), government bond issuance (bars: left scale), and outstanding government bonds (shadowy background: right scale) since FY 1983, and the major economic events in chronological order, so that the critical situation of Japan's finances can be understood at a glance.

The upper line, rising steadily upward, is the expenditure. As long as the people are alive and the country is growing, it is natural for spending to increase. Otherwise, the children's generation will be expected to lead a thriftier life than their parents' generation and will live under a sense of economic pressure.

The lower line is the tax revenue, and the problem is that this has been declining since FY 1990, as mentioned above. In this sense, the Democratic Party of Japan's "sorting" of the budget was misguided in terms of the nature of the problem. The reason is that no matter how much wasteful spending is curbed, it will be difficult to eliminate the budget deficit unless tax revenues increase. Also, the decision to raise the consumption tax rate to 8% was made by the Yoshihiko Noda administration of the DPJ. The consumption tax hike seems to be the consensus of almost all politicians capable of governing Japan.

Anyhow, during the "bubble economy," indicated by arrows at the bottom of the graph, both spending and tax revenue increased. However, as I mentioned earlier, the "Izanami boom" was only a long period of time and did not produce much economic expansion, but it did not contribute anything at all in terms of tax revenue, which eventually declined significantly.

It is obvious that if spending increases and tax revenues decrease, the budget deficit will increase. The bars show the amount of new government bonds issued, indicating that the government has borrowed money because it cannot live with the deficit. And the shadowy background shows the outstanding amount of government bonds, the amount of debt that has been piling up.

And the expenditure of 160.3 trillion yen on the far right reflects the compensation for the loss of economic activity halted by the counter-Corona measures. Tax revenue was projected to be 63.5 trillion yen, so the new debt was expected to be 90.2 trillion yen. Nevertheless, I have already mentioned that while the expenditure was revised upward to 175.7 trillion yen, the tax revenue forecast was revised downward to 60.8 trillion yen, so the new debt is expected to be over 112 trillion yen.

The events listed in chronological order below Chart 05 show that even crises that directly hit Japan, such as the Plaza Accord (Note: Cooperative measures to induce yen appreciation approved at a meeting of the G5 nations), were survived by Japan at the time. On the other hand, Japan, which was weakened by the consumption tax, was also hit hard by crises originating in other countries, such as the Asian currency crisis and the Lehman shock, and was left behind in economic growth even after the original countries of crises recovered.

I am hoping that the fact that we have been pushed to this point will make people realize that the only way out of the crisis is to change the tax system to one that leads to increased tax revenue. Japan cannot afford another consumption tax hike, which would obviously lead to a slowdown in the economy and a decrease in total tax revenue. Japan's government is no longer in a state of mere poverty, but in a state of virtual bankruptcy, and there is no way to improve it if the current situation continues.

6. The miracle of the world economy has changed from Japan to China

Table 01: GDP of the top 10 economies in 1989, vs. 2019 (Source: UN Statistics Division)

Country/Area	Year	Unit	Gross Domestic Product (GDP)
Brazil	1989	US$	375,484,929,930
Brazil	2019	US$	1,847,795,847,231
Canada	1989	US$	567,215,985,473
Canada	2019	US$	1,741,496,789,532
China, People's Republic of	1989	US$	456,287,003,694
China, People's Republic of	2019	US$	14,342,933,964,680
France	1989	US$	1,025,162,972,813
France	2019	US$	2,715,518,274,227
Germany	1989	US$	1,399,040,146,029
Germany	2019	US$	3,861,123,558,039
Italy	1989	US$	928,625,859,402
Italy	2019	US$	2,003,576,145,498
Japan	1989	US$	3,054,913,797,217
Japan	2019	US$	5,082,465,810,911
Spain	1989	US$	414,777,982,046
Spain	2019	US$	1,393,490,524,518
United Kingdom of Great Britain and Northern Ireland	1989	US$	926,926,143,222
United Kingdom of Great Britain and Northern Ireland	2019	US$	2,826,441,791,137
United States	1989	US$	5,641,580,000,000
United States	2019	US$	21,433,226,000,000
World	1989	US$	20,686,577,511,695
World	2019	US$	87,445,260,827,724

Table 01 shows the GDP of the 10 top economies in 1989, aligned with their GDP in 2019. The order is alphabetical and the figures are adjusted for the current US dollar. It was noted above that while Japan grew only 1.66 times in the 30 years since 1989, the world grew 4.23 times.

If we sort the 10 top economies in 1989 into the size of the economy in 2019, the 30-year growth rates are as follows: U.S. 3.80 times, China 31.43 times, Japan 1.66 times, Germany 2.76 times, UK 3.05 times, France 2.65 times, Italy 2.16 times, Brazil 4.92 times, Canada 3.07 times, and Spain 3.36 times. Compared to the world average of 4.23 times, the growth rate of developed countries is sluggish, with Japan being by far the most inferior. On the other hand, China's growth rate is literally off by a digit, overtaking Japan and leaving it far behind, while Japan was almost at a standstill.

Chart 06: GDP of the top 10 economies in 1989, vs. 2019 (Source: UN Statistics Division)

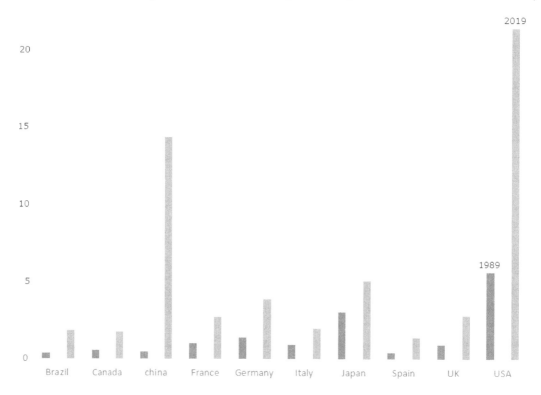

Chart 06 shows the nominal GDPs of the ten countries seen in Table 01 for 1989 and 2019, arranged alphabetically from left to right. The left side bars of each pair represent nominal GDP in 1989, and the right side bars of them represent nominal GDP in 2019. Japan, the world's second largest economy in 1989, was 53% the size of the U.S. economy, but by 2019, its share had dropped to 24%. China has replaced it as the world's second largest economy, and is now 2.82 times the size of Japan.

Some people may reckon this rapid growth is owing to the appreciation of the yuan. I suspected this myself, so I checked the figures from the United Nations Statistics Division.

Chart 07: China's nominal GDP trend in yuan and dollars, 1989-2019 (Source: UN Statistics Division)

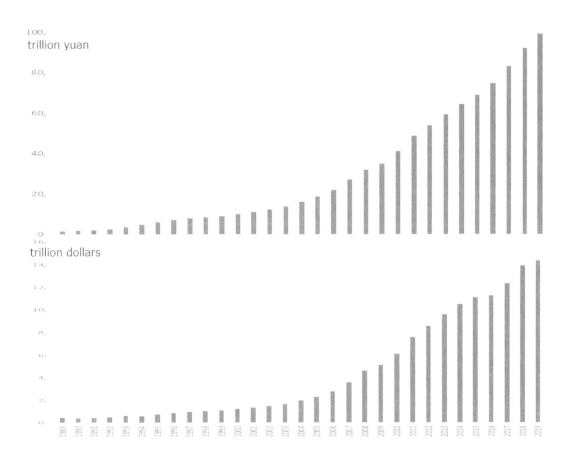

Chart 07 shows the trend of China's nominal GDP from 1989 to 2019 in both yuan and U.S. dollars. We can see that nominal GDP in 2019 approached 100 trillion yuan and exceeded 14 trillion dollars. The growth rates were 56.7 times and 31.4 times, respectively. From this chart, we don't need to look at the chart of the dollar-yuan exchange rate to see that the Chinese yuan has become weaker rather than stronger during this period.

We can say "The miracle of the world economy has changed from Japan to China." The Chinese have said they learned why Japan had suddenly changed from a miracle to a mystery. I won't go into this here because it is beyond the scope of this book, but it is something like if you accept the advice of other countries and lose sight of yourself, you will not be able to achieve healthy growth. The chart also shows that China has successfully escaped from the foreign pressures that Japan has suffered from the strong yen.

I don't think the Japanese system is great, and I'm sure there are plenty of things wrong with it that could be improved. But on the other hand, I don't think the systems of other countries are much better than Japan's. The declining birthrate and aging population is another problem common to most developed countries. However, while most of the world's economies have been growing steadily, Japan's economy has remained at its peak in 1997. And Japan's tax revenues can be said to have actually peaked in FY 1990.

Chart 08: Trends in nominal GDP in Japan and the world (Source: United Nations Statistics Division)

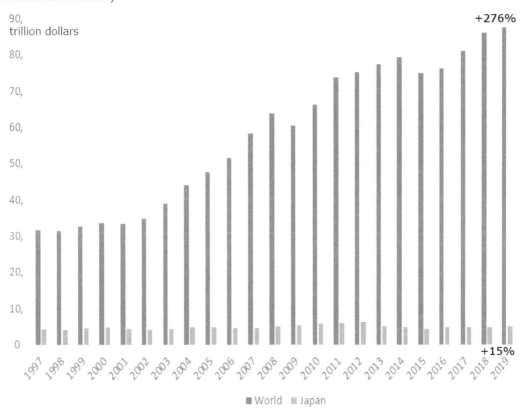

Chart 08 shows the nominal GDP in dollars for Japan and the world from 1997, when the Japanese economy first peaked, to 2019. During this period, the world grew by 276%, while Japan grew by only 15%.

In other words, it can be said that Japan's economic downfall began when it started trying to globalize and adopt other countries' systems. Nevertheless, I believe that what specifically destroyed the Japanese economy was the tax system, which gave up expecting an increase in tax revenue.

I remember the poster of Mr. Abe when he came to power for his second term. It read, "Restore Japan." At the time, I thought it meant the glorious Japanese economy of the past, so I had some hope for him.

However, Mr. Abe has left behind only his personal accomplishments, a slew of scandals, two consumption tax hikes, a stagnant economy, and the aforementioned major problems that he created and then threw away halfway through, leaving the next generation to deal with them. We have heard that he is seeking a third term, but is he really that stupid? It is hard to believe that someone who ran away once would take on a situation that has deteriorated to this point.

Table 02 below shows Table 01, which is the GDP of the top 10 economies in 1989, aligned with that of 2019, reworked into GDP per capita.

Table 02: GDP per capita of top 10 economies in 1989, vs. 2019 (Source: UN Statistics Division)

Country/Area	Year	Unit	Gross Domestic Product (GDP)
Brazil	1989	US$	2,566
Brazil	2019	US$	8,755
Canada	1989	US$	20,869
Canada	2019	US$	46,550
China, People's Republic of	1989	US$	394
China, People's Republic of	2019	US$	10,004
France	1989	US$	17,693
France	2019	US$	40,319
Germany	1989	US$	17,786
Germany	2019	US$	46,232
Italy	1989	US$	16,283
Italy	2019	US$	33,090
Japan	1989	US$	24,625
Japan	2019	US$	40,063
Spain	1989	US$	10,603
Spain	2019	US$	29,816
United Kingdom of Great Britain and Northern Ireland	1989	US$	16,269
United Kingdom of Great Britain and Northern Ireland	2019	US$	41,855
United States	1989	US$	22,591
United States	2019	US$	65,134
World	1989	US$	3,951
World	2019	US$	11,339

Japan's GDP per capita in 1989, seen in Table 02, was 6.23 times that of the world, including the poorest countries, but by 2019, it had dropped to 3.53 times. On the other hand, China's GDP per capita, a miracle in terms of economic size, jumped from 10.0% of the world's GDP to 88.2%, but still below the world. Considering that the number of Chinese billionaires according to the 2020 Census of Billionaires is 342, the second largest in the world, it may be said that the reality of China's version of socialism is that it has significantly widened the gap between the rich and the poor.

7. What is the real contribution of Abenomics?

Chart 09: Trends in unemployment rate (Source: Compiled from data of the Statistics Bureau of the Ministry of Internal Affairs and Communications)

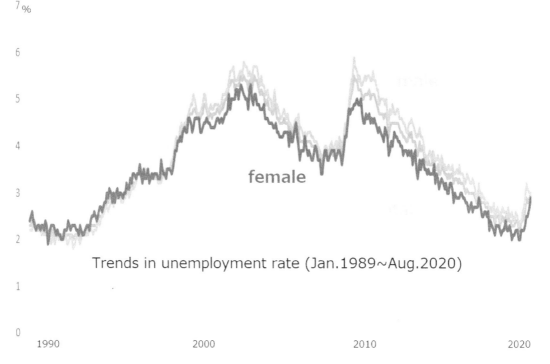

Chart 09 shows the monthly unemployment rate since 1989. The light line is the unemployment rate for men, the dark line is the unemployment rate for women, and the midline is the total unemployment rate for men and women. The left side shows that the unemployment rate for men was lower than that for women, but since the consumption tax hike in 1997 and the financial crisis in Japan, the rate for men has become higher.

When former Prime Minister Abe decided to step down, it was reported that a senior official of the Ministry of Finance said, "The most significant contribution of the Abe administration was that it raised the consumption tax twice." I believe that the consumption tax hike has undermined Japan's social security system, but even if that is not the case, it is common knowledge that the consumption tax hike will hurt the economy. I mentioned in the preface that the author of Chart 00 at the Ministry of Finance dared to highlight the tax revenue of 60.1 trillion yen for FY 1990, so his intentions may be close to my view. But, do the senior officials at the Ministry of Finance think that it is the job of the prime minister of Japan to bring the economy into recession?

Whatever the perceptions of Ministry of Finance officials, the most commendable achievement of Abenomics from a macroeconomic perspective must be the decline in the unemployment rate. If we take the start of Abenomics as April 2013, when the Bank of Japan Kuroda began its unprecedented monetary easing, the unemployment rate at that time was 4.4% for men and 3.8% for women, for a total of 4.1% for men and women. By August 2020, the rates had fallen to 3.0%, 2.9%, and 3.0%, respectively. This is a great achievement. However, it was still a big step back from the lowest levels of 2.3%, 2.0%, and 2.2% in November 2019, respectively.

As mentioned earlier, the size of the economy expanded by Abenomics has shrunk to the original size. Tax revenues have increased, but spending has skyrocketed even faster than that, so instead of balancing the primary balance, the budget gap has significantly widened. If the unemployment rate continues to rise, he would lose everything. One can understand why Mr. Abe thought about resigning on the day he broke the record for consecutive terms in office.

I look at these things as if they were price movement charts, as I used to be a dealer. The essence of trading is to recognize the turning point of these ups and downs, buy when the upward turning is confirmed, and sell when the downward turning is confirmed. Regardless of whether the fundamentals are good or bad, if you repeat the process of selling after the market has crossed a hill and buying after it has crossed a valley, you will surely make a profit. The key is to identify such turning points.

This chart shows double tops, followed by confirmation that the market was over the hill, and support in the upper 3% range was also broken below, and the market was steadily lower until around the time of the consumption tax hike in October 2019. However, it started to reverse after bottoming out at 2% in November, which is also a support level. The current shape has just finished confirming the valley crossing and is now in an upward wave. The impact of stopping the economy with the counter-Corona measures was significant, and it is not clear how far the unemployment rate will rise in the future. Mr. Abe has successfully taken his "personal gain".

8. Transformation of employment condition

Chart 10: Changes in employment status (Source: Compiled from data of the Statistics Bureau of the Ministry of Internal Affairs and Communications)

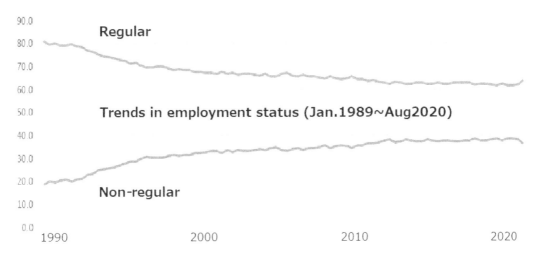

Chart 10 shows the ratio of regular and non-regular employment in the labor force from 1989 to 2020, which together is to be 100%. The upper line is for regular employment and the lower line is for non-regular employment.

From a macroeconomic point of view, the most commendable result of Abenomics must be the decline in the unemployment rate. At any rate, the number of jobs has increased, and for one time it has returned to near the level of 1990. But is it fair to say that the labor market has improved?

Chart 10 shows that around 1989, when the consumption tax was introduced, more than 80% of the workforce was in regular employment. This has been consistently replaced by non-regular employment. This trend has continued to develop under Abenomics. Recently, the ratio of regular employment has been increasing, and the reason for this can be clearly understood if we combine this chart with the previous chart 09. This means that in the economy that was hindered by the consumption tax hike and the counter-Corona measures that followed, it was mainly non-regular employment that greatly pushed up the unemployment rate.

In addition, as of the 2018 academic year, 86.1% of college students nationwide had part-time jobs, at least for a time (Japan Student Services Organization' Student Life Survey). The Corona pandemic, a natural threat, fell on the entire nation, but the government's measures against covid-19 directly hit these vulnerable people.

If we were to relate these employment figures to the stagnation of the Japanese economy and the decline in the competitiveness of Japanese companies, it would mean that if the ratio of regular employment falls, the competitiveness of companies will decline and the economy itself will stagnate.

In his book "The Challenge of Management," Sadamu Ichikura, known as "Japan's Drucker," wrote the following. (Reference: The Challenge of Management, author: Sadamu Ichikura, Nikkei BP, excerpted from p. 249 and p. 254)

What is the "function" of labor?
It is to create added value.

The interests of labor and management are perfectly aligned.

Since "value added is distributed to labor and management in a certain proportion," labor and management no longer need to fight over the distribution. And the only thing that works in both labor and management's favor is to increase the value added itself.

(Note: translated by Arata Yaguchi)

This implies that the creation of added value will be maximized if a compensation system is introduced in which the interests of labor and management are fully aligned.

In fact, when the Nihon Keizai Shimbun looked at the average annual salary of listed companies since Abenomics, it found that companies that have rewarded their human resources and increased their salaries have also seen their stock prices rise.

What all of this suggests is that the decline in the competitiveness of companies and the stagnation of the economy itself since around 1997 was partly due to the disregard of workers.

Some may argue that non-regular employment is not necessarily a choice on the part of companies, but rather a choice sometimes on employees who wish to have flexible working hours. However, given that it occurred at the same time as the recession and the rise in unemployment, it can be seen as the mainstream choice of companies that view labor as a cost.

Viewing labor as a cost is incompatible with "the interests of labor and management are perfectly aligned." This is because the interests of labor and management are in direct conflict, as lowering the cost increases the profit of the company. This means that the disregard for workers has been an impediment to the creation of added value in Japanese companies.

So what has been happening in terms of compensation? In the next section, we will take a look at wage trends.

9. Japan's real wages are diverging from the rest of the world

Chart 11: International comparison of real wage index trends (Source: All Japan Federation of Trade Unions)

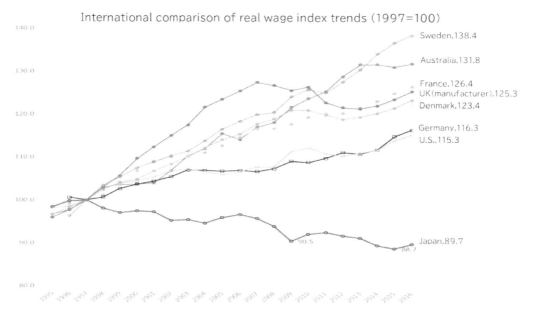

(Note: translated by Arata Yaguchi)

Chart 11 shows an international comparison of real wage trends since 1995. The lowest line shows Japan's real wages. The other lines are for major developed countries. It can be seen that while real wages have been rising to varying degrees in countries around the developed world, they have been declining only in Japan.

This chart is based on the year 1997, when Japan's real wages peaked, but you the readers of this book already know that 1997 was also the peak of the Japanese economy.

In the previous section, it was suggested that the shift in employment patterns from regular to non-regular employment has led to a deterioration in corporate performance. In light of the fact that real wages continued to fall during the same period, it becomes apparent that the disregard for workers, who are regarded as a cost, led to the deterioration of corporate performance. This led to a contraction in business investment and a decline in the purchasing power of workers, which in turn led to the economic recession.

But this doesn't tell us which came first, the recession or the disregard for workers, and which spiraled into making Japan poorer. It's a matter of "which came first: the chicken or the egg".

However, you the readers must also know that 1997 was the year the consumption tax rate was raised from 3% to 5%. If we go through such causal relationships, we can see that it all started with the introduction of the consumption tax in 1989 and the increase in the tax rate in 1997. In other words, the consumption tax caused an economic recession through sluggish consumer spending and deteriorating corporate performance, which in turn led to labor cost cuts. After that, it was a death spiral.

Now we know that the consumption tax has turned Japan from prosperity to collapse. Also, as a result of the Japanese people becoming poorer, department stores, etc., which had mainly targeted the middle class and above, declined, and the era of discount stores, including one dollar stores, has arrived.

Then the department stores relied on tax-free inbound consumption. Indeed, as incomes in other countries have continued to rise, they have been able to go abroad and shop. Nevertheless, even if department stores make profit from inbound consumption, corporate taxes are low, as mentioned above, and they are originally exempt from inbound consumption taxes. Therefore this does not increase the tax revenue that promises to maintain the social security system.

In Chart 11, while real wages in other countries continue to increase steadily, only Japan's wages decrease. This divergence was also seen in Chart 01 above. This is because tax revenue has been decreasing while spending has been increasing. This led to a sharp increase in the budget deficit and an ever-increasing public debt. This fork in the road for Japan's finances came in FY 1990, the year after the introduction of the consumption tax. In general, from a macroeconomic perspective, Japan became a completely different country after 1989. And it was around 1997 that this was decided. The consumption tax has been a key factor in the downfall of the Japanese economy in many aspects.

10. Turning point for nominal wages also coincides with consumption tax hike

Chart 12: Trends in wages (Source: Ministry of Health, Labour and Welfare)

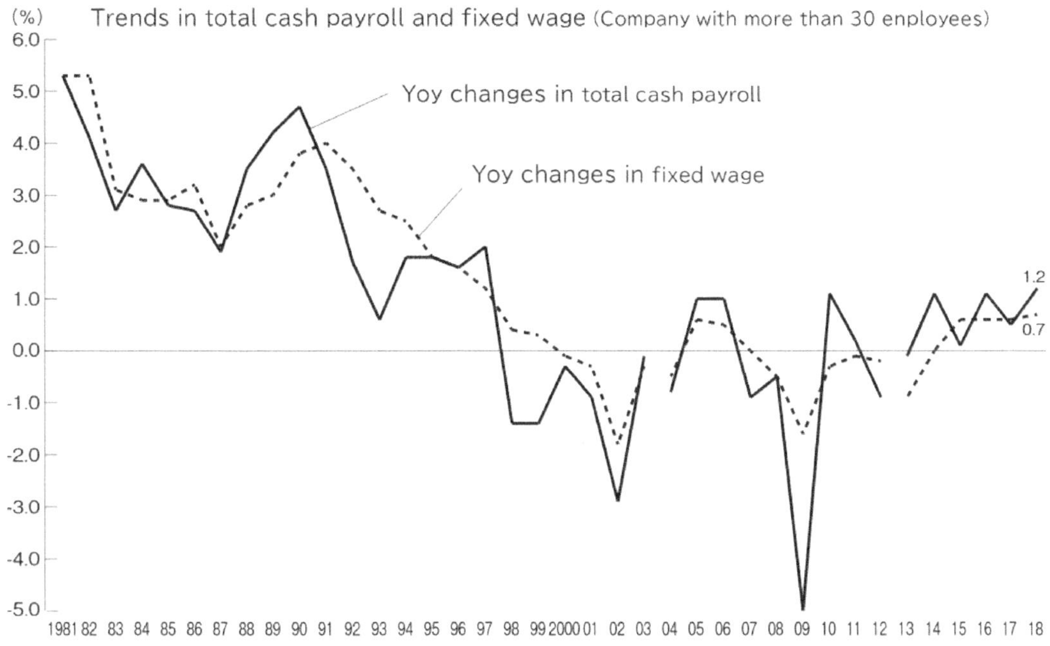

(Note: translated by Arata Yaguchi)

Chart 12 shows the nominal wages in Japan from 1981 to 2018, showing the year-on-year increase and decrease. The solid line shows the total cash payroll, and the dotted line shows the predetermined payroll. The predetermined payroll, or fixed wage, refers to base salary. It does not include bonuses or overtime pay.

Nominal wages are total cash payrolls, and even though payrolls increase, if the rate of inflation exceeds the rate of the increase, employees will be poorer in real terms. Therefore, the real wages shown in the previous Chart 11 are the total cash wages adjusted by the inflation rate. Chart 11 shows the decline in real wages in Japan. However, even though total cash payrolls increased, if the inflation rate rose more than that, real wages would decline. In other words, we cannot tell the increase or decrease in total cash payrolls from the previous Chart 11 alone.

Chart 12 shows that both total cash payrolls, represented by the solid line, and predetermined payroll, represented by the dotted line, have basically continued to decline. As you see later in the decline in the inflation rate from Chart 19 below, we know that the decline in nominal wages has been more than the decline in real wages.

However, while the previous Chart 11 indexes the real wages of 1997 as 100, Chart 12 shows the increase or decrease compared to the previous year. This means that wages tend to decrease in the year following a sharp increase in the previous year, and increase in the year following a sharp decrease in the previous year.

As a practical example, Chart 12 shows that the nominal wages for 2009 was -5% compared to the previous year. If 2008 was indexed to 100, the index for 2009 would be 95, and 2010 was 1% higher than the previous year. This means that the index for 2010 was 95 + 95 X 0.01, or just under 96, which is still more than 4 percentage points lower than the 100 of two years ago.

To confirm this, please take a look at the previous Chart 11. This chart has been adjusted for inflation, but it still shows that 2010 has not yet recovered the level of 2008. The "bottoming out" of wages, as seen in Chart 12, is a bit of graphical magic.

I dare not include the consumption tax arrow in this Chart 12; please look at 1989, 1997, and 2014. It can be seen that the drop in total cash payrolls, including bonuses and overtime pay, is larger than that in predetermined payroll. This means that bonuses and overtime pay reflect the economic downturn more strongly.

This also suggests that non-regular employment is more affected by the economic downturn than regular employment.

11. Money supply has increased 11.2 times since 1997

Chart 13: Trends in the size of the economy and the money supply (Source: Compiled from data of the Cabinet Office and the Bank of Japan)

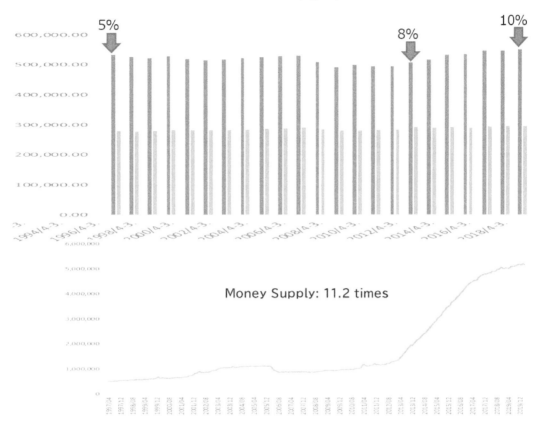

Chart 13 shows the relation between the size of the economy and the money supply from FY 1997 to FY 2019. The long bars show the change in nominal GDP, and the short bars show the change in personal consumption. The line chart below shows the Bank of Japan's money supply over the same period. It is clear that the money supply, which was less than 10% of the size of the economy in 1997, has now exceeded the size of the economy.

In considering the maintenance of the social security system, it is not acceptable to bypass the achievements and problems of Abenomics. This is because if Abenomics has been effective in maintaining the existence of the social security system, then subsequent governments will need to continue it. On the other hand, if, as I believe, it has jeopardized the survival of the social security system, it is necessary to quickly change course.

The economic expansion and increase in tax revenue that we have seen so far due to Abenomics has been back to square one. This strongly suggests that it only forced itself to make up numbers, and not the right direction.

Although the unemployment rate declined under Abenomics, the percentage of non-regular employment increased, and both nominal and real wages declined. Nevertheless, as I mentioned above, it is fair to say that both the size of the economy and tax revenues have temporarily reached new peaks. In my view, it was the money supply that contributed the most to this record breaking. In other words, it was quantitative easing that broke the record by force.

The size of the economy is the amount of money, such as 500 trillion yen, that represents the vital activities of the people, such as production or spending. If we increase the amount of currency, we should be able to assume that the prices of goods and services indicated by the currency, as well as the numerical value of the size of the economy as a result of these transactions, will also increase, even if only in a pretense.

However, while the volume of currency has increased rapidly, the size of the economy has remained almost flat. Since both graphs are from zero to 600 trillion yen, the difference appears to stand out as it is without any exaggeration. Normally, the size of the economy should be much larger than it is.

A possible reason is that much of the money may not have been spent. In fact, the short bars showing consumer spending seen in Chart 13 is flat. We also know that both households and businesses have been building up their bank deposits and cash reserves. On the other hand, what the previous Charts 11 and 12 showed was that the households of ordinary workers have not received the currency in spite of the fact that the country as a whole has been filled with affluent money. Even less has been given to part-time workers.

What this suggests is that the gap between the rich and the poor is widening. It also suggests that the widening gap is the reason why the economy stagnates. This will be discussed later.

12. The Bank of Japan "only sees prices"

Chart 14: Trends in Japan's official interest rates (Source: Bank of Japan data)

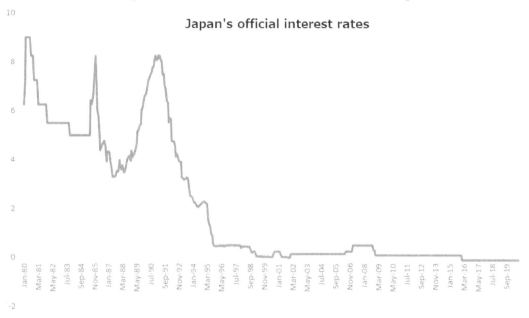

Chart 14 shows the trend of Japan's policy interest rates since 1980. Sometimes the policy rate in Japan was the "base discount rate and base lending rate (official discount rate)" and sometimes it was the overnight call rate. There was also a period from April 2013 to December 2015 when the Bank of Japan Kuroda did not place a policy rate. Currently, it refers to the interest rate charged on the policy rate balance in the current account. The current policy rate is minus 0.1 percent.

The Kuroda BOJ has supported Abenomics in terms of monetary policy. The Bank of Japan's website clearly states, "The Bank of Japan is the central bank of Japan, with the objective of achieving price stability and financial system stability."

The specific inflation target of the Kuroda BOJ is to stabilize at around 2%. The U.S. central bank, the Federal Reserve Bank (FRB), has the same inflation target, but the FRB has another major mission: to stabilize the job market.

If I had to pick just one thing as the most important objective of a country's economic policy, I would say that it should be "job market stability". This is because if there is a job for almost every citizen who wants a job, the economy and tax revenue will be stable, and it will likely be easier to maintain the social security system. It would also lead to a greater sense of well-being.

Nevertheless, the concern that arises with full employment is inflation. When both economic growth and income growth increase at a steady rate, the prices of goods and services will come under upward pressure. And once inflation overtakes the rate of economic growth and income growth, the purchasing power for the same amount of money will in turn decrease, and the country will become poorer in real terms. For this reason, real GDP is defined as nominal GDP (gross domestic product) minus the inflation rate, and real wages are defined as nominal wages (total cash payroll) minus the inflation rate.

The U.S. Federal Reserve Bank considers "job market stability" and "price stability" to be the two missions of its monetary policy because they are connected to the objective of the country's economic policy, which is to enhance the welfare of its citizens. The FRB has set as its ideal and goal that the U.S. economy remains close to full employment while prices remain stable at around 2 percent. Monetary policy and fiscal policy, supporting each other, play a major role in the country's economic policy.

On the other hand, the Bank of Japan's objectives are "price stability" and "financial system stability". Although it has stated so, the Bank of Japan has effectively abandoned "financial system stability."

Since the Suga administration came to power, it has been stressed that there are too many regional banks and that their earnings are not rising. However, it has been repeated many times, even in the BOJ's own statement, that the negative interest rate policy is hurting banks' profits. The Financial Services Agency of Japan has continued to make the same point. This shows that megabanks and regional banks have been the victims of the central bank's policies. In other words, the stability of the financial system has been shaken by the policies of the Bank of Japan.

This is not only the case in Japan. In fact, banks in the Eurozone and other countries with negative interest rate policies are all struggling to make ends meet. Their core business of lending is basically in the red, and they are looking for other sources of revenue.

To take an example, in September 2020, Sumitomo Mitsui Banking Corporation became the first Japanese company to issue a negative yield corporate bond in the European market. The bonds were covered bonds (bonds secured by mortgage bonds) with a funding amount of 1 billion Euros and a maturity of 5 years, carrying a face interest rate of 0.01%, and were issued at a price of 100.895 Euros per 100 Euros of face value. Therefore, SMBC was able to raise funds at -0.168% in real terms. This is because bonds can be bought at a price above par (100), but will only be returned at 100 when redeemed.

In other words, although this bond has a positive interest rate of +0.01% per year, it is very small. So, if the purchaser pays the bond at a price of 100.895 and gets it back at a lower price of 100, he or she will not make up for the loss of 0.895. Therefore, the purchaser will have an annualized -0.168% negative yield. In other words, SMBC can earn a positive yield while borrowing money because the buyer pays for the trading loss that it knows in advance.

The buyers of SMBC bonds are the banks in the Eurozone, and since the ECB has introduced a negative interest rate policy, if the banks deposit their surplus funds with the ECB, they will incur an interest rate of -0.5%. While they invest the funds in corporate bonds issued by SMBC, the yield will be negative, but the loss will be relatively small. This is a substantial benefit to a specific party, and would normally be considered an unfair transaction, but the central bank is leading the way.

In this deal, a loss is a loss even if the amount of loss is small. This means that stable profits cannot be expected in this environment of ultra-low interest rates, and even if profits are made, they cannot even cover the cost of personnel and other expenses. The ultra-low interest rate policy, not to mention the negative interest rate policy, makes it difficult for banks to operate and undermines the stability of the financial system.

However, as seen in Chart 14, Japan's policy rate last touched 0.51% in March 1997 and has remained below 0.50% since then.

This means that "The Bank of Japan is the central bank of Japan, with the objective of achieving price stability and financial system stability." mentioned on the BOJ's website, was the statement of the past BOJ, when I used to talk with the people in charge. And the current BOJ, or BOJ after FY 1997, is actually "only looking at prices.

13. The gap between banks' deposits and loans is 290 trillion yen

Chart 15: Japanese banks' loan-to-deposit ratio and loan-to-deposit gap (Source: Okasan Securities)

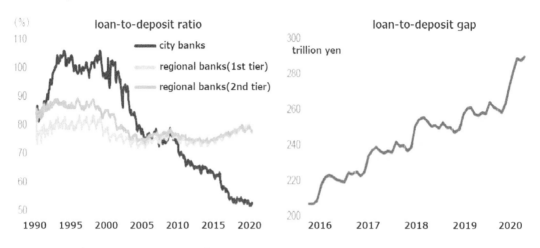

(Note: translated by Arata Yaguchi)

Chart 15 is compiled by Okasan Securities based on data from the Bank of Japan. The left side charts show the loan-to-deposit ratio from January 1990 to July 2020. The dark line is for city banks, the light lines are for 1st tier regional banks and for 2nd tier regional banks. The chart on the right shows the trend in the loan-deposit gap for banks from January 2016 to August 2020.

The loan-to-deposit ratio is the ratio of outstanding loans to outstanding deposits. From the charts on the left, we can see that the overall ratio has been declining steadily, that is, the ratio of loans has been decreasing.

The loan-deposit gap is the balance of deposits minus the balance of loans, and we can see that the loan-deposit gap has been increasing as the loan-deposit ratio has been declining. Does this mean that banks are reluctant to lend even though they have more than enough resources to do so?

Banks are engaged in indirect finance. Their business is to pool surplus funds collected as deposits from customers and lend them out to those who need the funds. By borrowing at a lower interest rate and lending at a higher rate, they try to make a profit, which can be regarded as an intermediary fee. The reluctance to lend is not due to a lack of need for profit, but when the credit risk is not worth it.

Normally, loans to individuals are considered riskier than loans to large corporations due to higher possibility of default and delinquent interest payments.

Nevertheless, at one time, banks expanded consumer loans to the point where the authority considered them problematic because the banks believed they could get enough interest rates that were commensurate with the credit risk. Even with the prospect of some loan losses, they were willing to lend because they saw the high interest rate consumer loans as profitable. The reason why this was seen as a problem was because the banks ignored the conditions of the consumers and inflated the loans for their own needs, which led to a number of complaints from the consumers.

This strongly suggests that banks are willing to increase lending as much as they can if it will lead to profits without the Bank of Japan going out of its way to encourage the circulation of funds to the market through its ultra-low interest rate policy. This is because banks are suffering from a surplus of money and investment difficulties.

Chart 15 shows that as of August 2020, banks have about 290 trillion yen in surplus funds. This is because lending growth is not keeping pace with deposit growth. In particular, city banks have loan assets only about half of the size of their deposits, suggesting that they are relying on other sources of revenue. That is a good contrast to the pre-2000 period when they were lending more than they had in deposits.

On the left side of Chart 15, in the chart of loan-to-deposit ratio, you can see the typical movement of the city banks in the dark line. From 1990 to 1994-95, lending will increase in line with the bursting of the bubble economy and economic slowdown. It then peaked for the second time around 1998.

What can be seen here is that the loan-deposit ratio around 1990 was around 80%. Although the involvement of companies specializing in housing finance in the formation of the bubble economy is well known, this chart suggests that banks may not have been very much involved in the formation of the bubble economy, including loans to such non-banks. Rather, the chart suggests that banks may have taken on too much credit risk, with their loan-to-deposit ratio exceeding 100%, by providing financing to companies whose performance deteriorated after the bubble burst.

This is because in 1997, when the loan-to-deposit ratio was near its peak, the Nippon Credit Bank and the Hokkaido Takushoku Bank went bankrupt. The following year, in 1998, the Long-Term Credit Bank of Japan also failed. Of course, each bank has its own reasons for failing, but it is interesting to note that the loan-to-deposit ratio was over 100% when these top-ranked banks failed one after another.

However, after the year 2000, the loan-to-deposit ratio began to decline sharply. What will the readers make of this? Looking at it from this perspective alone, one might think that the Bank of Japan had no choice but to introduce ultra-low interest rate policies because those banks had become discouraged by credit risk and stopped pumping money into the market.

However, the trend in the policy rate shown in Chart 14 above indicates that the Bank of Japan continued to cut interest rates from the economic slowdown that began in 1990, so that by 1997, when Japan was experiencing negative growth, the rate was below 0.50%, leaving little room for rate cuts. If we look at this together with the loan-deposit ratio in Chart 15, we can see that lending grew during the period of interest rate cuts, but declined after interest rates became ultra-low.

Since making a profit from lending would be extremely difficult under ultra-low or negative interest rate policies, the BOJ's policy is to "deny banks the ability to make sufficient profit from lending," which is their primary business. This is what has led to the decline in the loan-to-deposit ratio and the rise in the loan-to-deposit gap, as seen in Chart 15. In other words, the Bank of Japan's policies have made it impossible for banking businesses to make enough profit.

However, the policy rate is a reference rate for financial institutions and has nothing to do directly with lending to corporations and individuals. Nevertheless, the reason for setting a base rate is that lending rates based on the base rate, with an additional premium depending on the term and creditworthiness, are applied to corporations and individuals. This means that since the interest rate considered risk-free has never exceeded 0.5% since March 1997, it has become difficult to secure sufficient profits even by adding interest rate premiums based on term and creditworthiness. Thus, the ultra-low interest rate policy has made banking a structurally depressed business.

The reversal of the loan-to-deposit ratio between city and regional banks seen in Chart 15 above suggests that city banks, having lost domestic sources of profitability, have begun to take on what can be called excessive overseas risk. On the other hand, regional banks are not required to report to the BIS (Bank for International Settlements), but instead have to specialize in domestic operations, so they have no way to escape overseas. As a result, they have continued to lend even when they are not making enough profit, as can be seen from the fact that their loan-to-deposit ratio has not declined. And this resulted in them being cornered profitably to the extent that they were forced to restructure.

This indicates that city banks are currently extremely vulnerable to future deterioration in overseas credit risk, while regional banks are extremely vulnerable to future deterioration in domestic credit risk. I use the word "extremely" because it is highly likely that they are taking "excessive risk" because under the negative interest rate policy, they will not be able to generate profits from their normal risk operations.

The trend in the policy rate shown in Chart 14 and the trends in the loan-to-deposit ratio and the loan-to-deposit gap shown in Chart 15 suggest that the Bank of Japan's ultra-low interest rate policy, which is supposed to promote the circulation of funds, has not been working. Here, continuing to pursue a policy that does not work will only mean that the negative effects will continue to increase.

14. Introduction of negative interest rate policy

Chart 16: Japanese government bond yield curve (Source: Compiled from Ministry of Finance data)

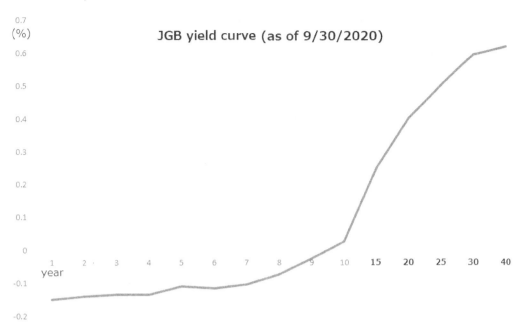

Chart 16 shows the yield curve of Japanese government bonds as of the end of September 2020. The yield curve connects the yield levels from short-term to long-term, in this case from 1-year to 40-year JGBs. The yield is a percentage of the increase in investment capital, and usually refers to the average yield per year.

For example, if you buy a 1-year JGB at the end of September 2020 for 1,001,490 yen at the market price, it will be redeemed one year later at the end of September 2021 for face per value of 1 million yen, resulting in a yield of minus 0.149%. Chart 16 shows that the yield will be negative from 1-year to 9-year JGBs.

The fact that banks have become a structurally depressed industry and the stability of the financial system has been undermined becomes more serious after the introduction of the negative interest rate policy in January 2016. Negative interest rates are like putting the cart before the horse where lenders pay interest rates to borrowers, so that borrowers make more money the more they borrow, and lenders lose a lot of money when they lend more. Considering that banks are the leading lenders in the economy, this means that the central bank has introduced a policy of bullying banks.

The policies of Abenomics were meant to encourage people to "take more risks," but this would have the opposite effect if the returns from the short-term financial instruments market were eliminated. Short-term financial instruments are a safety net for fund management, and if the returns from these instruments are positive, fund managers can face greater risks. Even if risk-taking fails, the return from short-term financial instruments will compensate for it.

Back in the days when short-term interest rates offered decent positive yields, there was something called "forbidden T-bill buying" among bond dealers at financial institutions. T-bills are short-term certificates of obligation issued by the Treasury, discount bonds with maturities of 2, 3, 6 or 12 months. Discount bonds are issued at a discount and redeemed at face value, with no interest payments, and the trading profit becomes the yield.

For the sake of clarity, let's use a 1-year T-bill as an example. Suppose the yield is 2%, the T-bill is issued at 98 yen and redeemed at 100 yen. Whoever buys it will make a profit of 2 yen. In other words, it has nothing to do with the trading skills of the dealer, but if he buys a T-bill with a face value of 100 billion yen for 98 billion yen, he will make a capital gain of 2 billion yen with almost no risk (since it is the risk of his own government, it is considered risk-free). And that 2 billion yen will act as a safety net for risk-taking.

As a dealer, I used to deal huge amounts of money for a large company, and being a large company was a safety net for me. In such an environment, where failure would lead to the collapse of the company and the loss of many people's jobs, people with normal sense would shrink.

Chart 16 shows that the Japanese government bond market has no choice but to take a 10-year or longer time horizon risk if you want a positive yield. And when you look back at what happened in the world and what happened in Japan in the decade between 2010 and 2020, you will see that that is an extraordinary risk.

Since the introduction of the consumption tax in 1989, the risk has been about 30 years. When you invest 100 million yen for 30 years now, the return will be only 595,000 yen per year.

Alternatively, credit risk can be taken in the form of corporate bonds, which carry the risk of bankruptcy. In the U.S., on average, about 40% of funds can be recovered from bonds that have defaulted on their obligations. In the case of high-yielding bonds, a lot of interest is received before the failure, plus 40% of the face value could be recovered. This was the worst case scenario. However, in the bankruptcies after the Corona pandemic in 2020, it was reported that the recovery of funds averaged less than 1% by the end of September.

15. Abenomics has destroyed the interest rate market

Chart 17: Japanese government bond yield curve (Source: Compiled from Ministry of Finance data)

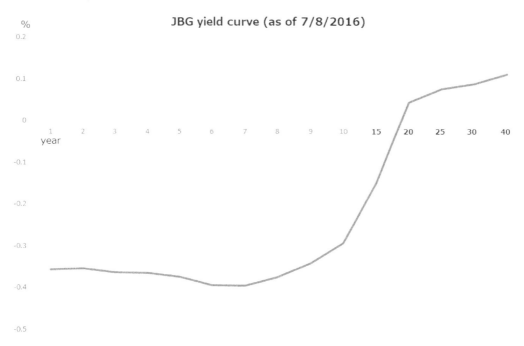

Chart 17 shows the yield curve of Japanese government bonds as of July 8, 2016. Here, we can see that up to 15-year JGBs have negative yields.

After the introduction of the negative interest rate policy in January 2016, the 10-year JGB, the benchmark for Japanese government bonds, posted a negative yield for the first time in history on February 24 of the same year. Since that time, it can be said that pension funds and life insurance companies, which are entrusted with our assets, have lost their core investment vehicles, which have no foreign currency exchange risk and the smallest credit risk in Japan. Long-term investors do not necessarily invest mainly in 10-year government bonds, but I mention them as a symbolic investment destination. This means that the government has taken away the safe investment vehicles from us.

It was on July 8 of the same year that Japan's 10-year JGB hit their lowest ever yield, at -0.293%. The yield curve for that day is shown in Chart 17 above. If you want a positive yield, you have no choice but to leave your money lying around for more than 20 years, and even so, the yield would not reach 0.1% in 30 years, which would not be enough to cover the cost of the investment management organization.

This means that the Bank of Japan's negative interest rate policy has not only denied banks to make profits from their lending operations, but also denied long-term investors to make profits from their JGB investments. You can see that Abenomics has effectively destroyed the interest rate market.

Nevertheless, investment institutions must also survive. Pension funds will not suffer sudden withdrawal of their funds, and by gradually lowering benefits, they will be able to avoid having their investment difficulties exposed. Life insurance companies can also survive without necessarily taking large risks, as long as they maintain a balance between premiums and claims payments.

Yet, for example, the GPIF (Government Pension Investment Fund), which manages 172.5 trillion yen of our pensions as of the end of September 2020, allocates half of its assets to foreign currencies and half of its yen assets to stocks. In other words, it holds a quarter each of foreign bonds, foreign stocks, domestic bonds, and domestic stocks.

Meanwhile, life insurers are investing more actively in foreign bonds than before. This means that they are increasing their overseas risk, just like city banks, because they no longer have a core domestic investment vehicle.

Japan Post Bank with more than 207 trillion yen in assets under management has about 85 trillion yen invested in foreign securities and other risky assets, and it has announced plans to expand this to about 90 trillion yen.

In addition, the number of "commitment line contracts" has increased rapidly among banks and other financial institutions in 2020. This is an agreement in which a bank makes a commitment to a company to provide a loan within a predetermined period and limit without examination, enabling the company to raise funds as needed. The advantage for the bank is that it earns a fee in addition to the interest rate.

According to the results of a survey conducted by Teikoku Databank, the number of listed companies that announced the signing of commitment line contracts between January 1 and September 30, 2020 increased 4.7 times from the previous year to 165, and the total contract amount increased 9.5 times to 3.146 trillion yen. This means that banks are taking on greater credit risk in exchange for fees.

The reason why there has been such a sharp increase of commitment line contracts during this period is obvious. Companies whose sales had plummeted due to businesses shut down as a result of counter-Corona measures were using them to secure cash flow for a reasonable period of time. This means that private companies, banks, and the government all decided to be in the same boat in the emergency situation of the Corona pandemic.

However, the loan-deposit gap of about 290 trillion yen shown in Chart 15 above tells us that, aside from the government, the banks and the private sector that have deposited funds with them still have excess capacity.

What is the big problem here? The counter-Corona measures have made it structurally impossible for companies to make money. The negative interest rate policy has made it structurally impossible for financial institutions to make money. The government has structurally abandoned the means to make money 30 years ago. This shows that all the problems have been created by the government.

What are the structural reforms that the Japanese economy is facing?

Without tax reform, we shall not be able to destroy this negative structure, shall we?

16. Income transfer from the private sector to the government

Chart 18: Trends in interest payment and interest rates (Source: Ministry of Finance)

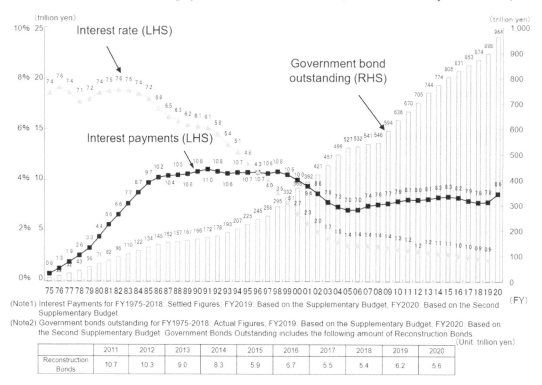

Chart 18 shows the outstanding amount of JGBs (bars), the level of interest rates (light line), and the interest payment cost (dark line) from FY 1975 to FY 2020. The outstanding balance multiplied by the interest rate is approximately the interest payment cost.

What we saw in the previous Chart 17 was that the yield on Japanese government bonds from 1 year to over 15 years was negative. Even at present, it is negative up to over 9 years. As a result, financial institutions ranging from banks and securities firms to pension funds and life insurance companies have lost their core investment vehicles that carry not much risk. This means that the general public, who invest their money in savings and short-term financial products and pay for pension and life insurance for their retirement, have lost their investment income.

On the other hand, every coin has its face and the back. If the general public and financial institutions, the private sector so to speak, are losing money, there must be somebody who is making money there.

The bars of outstanding government bonds in Chart 18 shows that the government's debt has been steadily accumulating. The reason for this, as mentioned earlier, is that tax revenues have rather decreased while expenditures have continued to increase. On the other hand, the light line shows that interest rates have been steadily declining. The reason for this is the continuation of the ultra-low interest rate policy for more than 20 years. As a result, the dark line has been in a flat to declining trend.

What this chart shows is that despite the rapid increase in the outstanding debt, the cost of interest payments has been declining. This shows that it is the Japanese government that has been profiting from the extremely low interest rate policy, which has had a very harmful effect on the private sector. This means a transfer of income from the private sector to the government, which is equivalent to tax collection in a different form. Again, this is a de facto tightening policy that siphons off funds from the private sector, suggesting that it may have been one of the factors that prolonged deflation.

What worries me, though, is the figure on the far right, which shows interest expenses at an 18-year high. This figure does not yet reflect the surge in government bond issuance for counter-Corona measures, but still with a lower bound on interest rate declines and the expansion of outstanding debt seemingly unstoppable, it is fair to assume that interest expenses have entered an upward trend.

This implies that the government itself has been cornered, even though it has been siphoning off funds from the private sector, just as total tax revenue has declined despite the introduction of the consumption tax. (I'm suggesting that the government itself has been cornered because of having siphoned off much funds from the private sector, just as the introduction of the consumption tax has caused a decline in total tax revenue, just as the disrespect for workers has resulted in a decline in corporate performance.) I see this as the government being trapped because it has sucked too much money out of the general public. Here, if interest expenses were to skyrocket, Japan's fiscal crisis is likely to materialize.

17. Price trends

Chart 19: Trends in the consumer price index (Source: Compiled from e-Stat data)

Chart 19 shows the trend of the CPI from 1980 to 2019, indexed with 2015 as the base year. It can be seen that prices have basically stayed down and have remained flat around zero. In paragraph 12 above, I explained that the Bank of Japan is currently "looking only at prices." Its price target is to stabilize at around 2 percent.

Although we have mentioned that the excessively low interest rate policy has had the de facto tightening effect of siphoning off funds from the private sector, interest rate cuts are still essentially a means of boosting the economy. In a disinflationary environment in which prices are falling, interest rate cuts are expected to stop prices from falling or even raise them. Moreover, as shown in Chart 13 above, the government has even supplied a large amount of funds since April 2013.

What this trend in the CPI shows is that prices, which should have risen under the ultra-low interest rate policy, have not risen easily. This strongly suggests that factors other than interest rates are pushing down prices. What happened at the four peaks seen in Chart 19, around 1990, 1997, 2008, and 2014, when prices that had fallen were held back in an attempt to rebound? Aren't these what are making Japan disinflationary?

As you the readers have been reading this far, you probably have guessed the answer.

18. Consumption tax hikes have led to disinflation

Chart 20: Trends in the consumer price index and the BOJ policy rate (Source: Compiled from e-Stat and Bank of Japan data)

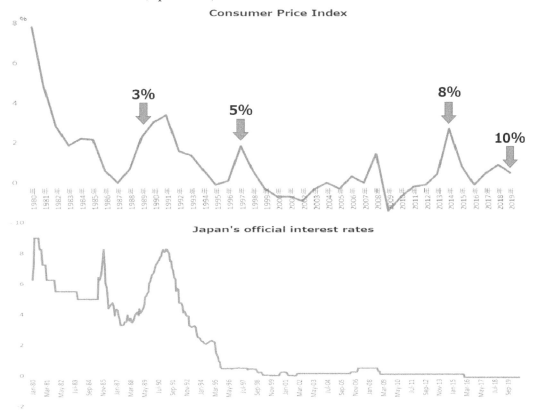

Chart 20 shows the trend of the consumer price index from 1980 to 2019 in the previous Chart 19, with the timing of hikes and the rates of the consumption tax, and lined up with the trend of the policy rate since 1980 in Chart 14 above.

In the lower part of the chart, when interest rates fall sufficiently, the prices in the upper part of the chart begin to show an upward trend, but when there is the consumption tax hike at the point where they are raised, it can be seen that they begin to fall again. Here again, the consumption tax hike coincided with the downward inflection point of the Japanese economy.

Of these five peaks in prices, the peak around 2008 is thought to be the impact of the Lehman shock. The consumption tax hike seems to have an impact comparable to that of the Lehman shock.

The trend of the policy rate since March 1997, seen in the lower part of Chart 20, shows that the policy rate had been sticking to the ring of almost zero interest rates (0% to 0.5%) in order to somehow raise consumer prices, but was finally forced out of the ring and fell into negative territory when the tax was raised to 8%.

This also illustrates a key challenge facing Japan's next generation. Monetary easing is no longer an option. Japan's future monetary policy will be neutral at best, with virtually no other option but to tighten.

What is likely to happen with tighter monetary policy is disinflation, recession, higher loan interest burden including JGB interest payment costs, and plummeting bond prices. This means that Japan's monetary policy is checkmated for a chess game and already no way out.

That is why I am appealing to you the readers in this book, believing that tax reform is the only thing left to do. The only people who can save the Japanese economy are the Japanese voters.

19. Consumption tax cannot cover social security costs

Chart 21-1: Breakout of general account budget for the fiscal year 2020 (from: Ministry of Finance)

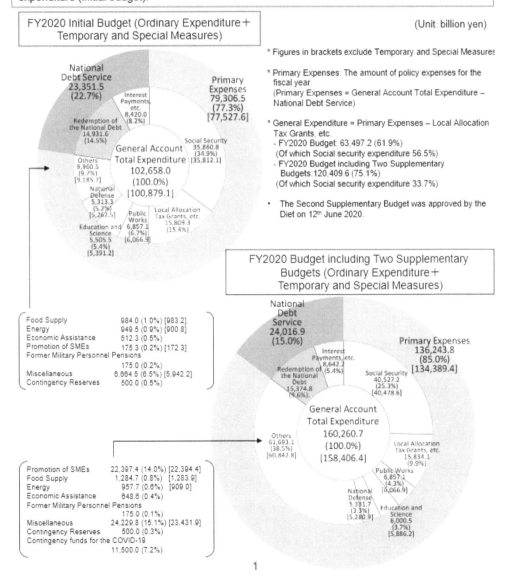

Chart 21-1 shows the breakdown of expenditures for FY 2020 on the Ministry of Finance's website, including the initial budget and the budget after the (second) supplementary budget due to the Corona pandemic. It can be seen that the original budget was 102.7 trillion yen, while the revised budget is 160.3 trillion yen. And the third supplementary budget, approved by the Cabinet on December 15, amounted to 175.7 trillion yen.

As we have seen so far in this book, tax revenues peaked immediately after the introduction of the consumption tax, and the size of the economy peaked immediately after the tax rate was raised. The consumption tax hike has also been linked to disinflation. The consumption tax hike advocated by politicians and bureaucrats is a massive risk.

So, even if we take that much risk, will raising the consumption tax really protect the social security system?

So far, it has turned out that the consumption tax revenue is Japan's largest source of revenue. The projected amount of the consumption tax revenue for FY 2020 was estimated to be 21.7 trillion yen, but since the projected total tax revenue is down, it is likely to be revised downward due to the significant drop in consumption caused by the Corona pandemic, no matter how stable a source of revenue it is. On the other hand, even if the economy improves in the future, there will not be a large upward swing due to the stable financial resources. Assuming that the consumption tax revenue is stable at slightly more than 20 trillion yen, will it be enough to finance the social security system?

According to Chart 21-1, social security expenditures paid by the government (as a subsidy for social insurance premiums) were 35.9 trillion yen in the original budget, but increased to 40.5 trillion yen due to the economic downturn caused by the Corona pandemic. This implies that social security expenditures increase when the economy worsens.

On the other hand, it is a well-known fact that the consumption tax is a factor in the economic downturn, which is evident from the numerous data we have mentioned. This strongly suggests that if the consumption tax is increased, social security costs will increase.

Now that the consumption tax is a stable source of revenue, the tax revenue to be gained from the tax hike can be predicted to some extent depending on the tax rate, but it is not necessarily the case that the increase in social security expenses due to the economic downturn will be contained within the scope of the increase in tax revenue. As seen in the supplementary budget due to the Corona pandemic, if it does not fall within this range in the future, the result will be the exact opposite of the original objective, which is to expand social security expenditures because of the consumption tax hike. In other words, the consumption tax will not be a source of revenue for social security, but rather it will increase social security expenditures, possibly jeopardizing the system.

In fact, it is undeniable that the introduction of the consumption tax and the increase in the tax rate may have led to an increase in social security expenditures. I personally believe that the consumption tax has reduced total tax revenue and increased social security expenditures.

As can be seen in Chart 21-1, social security spending is only a quarter of total expenditures. Still, it exceeds 40 trillion yen. This strongly suggests that the financial resources Japan should rely on are not the consumption tax, which is a stable source of slightly more than 20 trillion yen, but the income tax and corporate tax, which have the potential to rise significantly if the economy recovers. We cannot protect the system, when Japan's largest source of revenue is the consumption tax, which is a "stable source of revenue."

20. Debt-dependent finances

Chart 21-1: Breakout of general account budget for the fiscal year 2020 (from: Ministry of Finance)

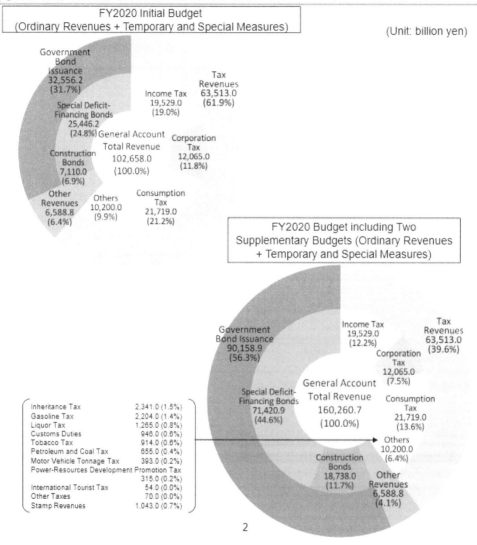

Chart 21-2, also from the Ministry of Finance's website, shows the breakdown of revenue for FY 2020, showing that the government is relying heavily on debt for its revenue. The generous spending on the counter-Corona measure was essential to support households and businesses in the midst of an existential crisis. But we can't get blood from a stone. We can say that this is a burden to the next generation.

The parents' generation up to the Abenomics era, including myself, will leave behind huge debts rather than assets for our descendants. In the case of individuals, there is the option of renunciation of inheritance, but this is not the case with national debt. Not only in the history of the world, but also in today's extremely poor countries, such debts are not metaphorical, but are life-threatening to the lives of the people.

Even though I myself have understood the meaning of the consumption tax for years, I regret that I have explained it only to a limited number of people. The Corona pandemic, which caused the budget deficit to exceed 110 trillion yen for a single fiscal year, made me feel the need to ask more people about it. If the next generation understands the meaning of the tax system and accepts the consumption tax hike, then so be it. However, I do not believe that you the readers have been given the materials to make a correct decision. That is why this book is intended to provide such information.

If the market is rising in a straight line, anyone can make money no matter where they buy. The only people who will lose money are those who sell. On the other hand, if the market is going down in a straight line, you can't just keep buying. Fortunately, in the market, the numbers tell you your profit and loss, so you don't have to hold on to your losses forever. If you can decide to sell double the position there, you can start to make profit from there.

How could we have come this far with tax revenues peaking at just over 60 trillion yen in FY 1990, FY 2018 and FY 2020, while spending over the past decade has generally hovered around 100 trillion yen and will exceed 175 trillion yen this fiscal year, and with a tax system that cannot be expected to increase tax revenues no matter how you calculate it? The figures clearly show us the error of our policy. The fiscal situation shown in Chart 01 above and its contents shown in Charts 21.1 and 21.2 suggest that the only way out is to drastically change the tax system, and that the time has finally come. A drastic change in the tax system means a return to the pre-1989 tax system.

The use of large sums of fiscal funds that have no way of being repaid can only be justified if it is accompanied by results. Even if the government overspends on currency, it can be forgiven for being "reckless" if the economy regains its strength while credit is maintained, and the budget deficit is eliminated as a result. However, in order to do so, the tax system must be restored to one that encourages economic growth, and one that increases tax revenue when growth occurs.

I have already mentioned that the tax revenue of 63.5 trillion yen shown in Chart 21-2 is expected to be revised downward to 60.8 trillion yen.

21. The introduction of the consumption tax was combined with the reduction in the corporate tax rate

Chart 22: Corporate profits, corporate tax rate, and corporate tax revenue (Source: written in Ministry of Finance data)

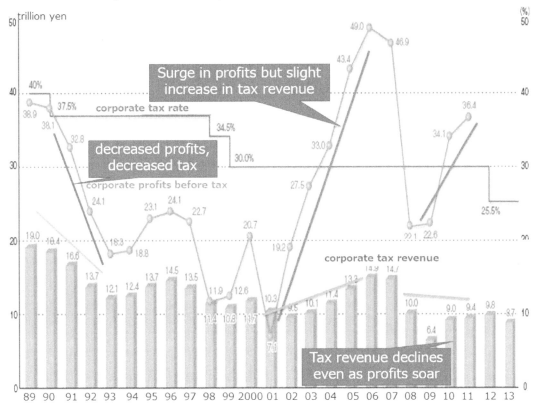

Chart 22 shows the trend of corporate profit before tax (light line with large swings), corporate tax rate (stair-step line), and corporate tax revenue (bars) from FY 1989 to FY 2013, with some notes added. The corporate tax is an income tax levied on corporations.

Did you the readers know, even before reading this book, that the introduction of the consumption tax in FY 1989 was paired with a corporate tax cut? That is a major reason why, as mentioned earlier, corporate tax revenue was only 65% of the FY 1989 level, despite the fact that corporate sales and corporate profits in FY 2018 were the largest ever.

Incidentally, a company is one that is legally recognized as having the same personality (juridical personality) as a human being. The company was invented in England in the 16th century, which separated the debts of a business from those of an individual. This was later used as a stock company to finance the Age of Exploration. Typical examples of corporations are general companies, private schools, pension organizations, and labor unions.

According to the National Tax Agency's website, the current corporate tax rate for ordinary corporations (joint stock companies, limited partnership companies, special limited liability companies, medical corporations, mutual companies, and corporate partnerships under the Commercial Code, as well as general incorporated associations and general incorporated foundations) is 23.2%. This is the same for FY 2018, and corporate tax revenue for the year was 12.3 trillion yen.

The corporate tax rate was 40% in FY 1989, when corporate tax revenue peaked at 19 trillion yen. If the tax rate had been 40% in FY 2018, corporate tax revenue would have been 21.2 trillion yen, which would have been a record high along with record sales and profits.

As mentioned above, economic growth will decelerate from FY 1990, the year after the introduction of the consumption tax, to FY 1997. Then, from FY 1997, when the consumption tax rate was raised to 5%, economic growth became negative.

Corporate profits in Chart 22 plummeted from 38.9 trillion yen in FY 1989 (shown on the left) to 18.3 trillion yen in FY 1993. Since the tax rate was also reduced from 40% to 37.5%, tax revenue declined from 19.0 trillion yen to 12.1 trillion yen. This was a natural move as the worsening of profits due to the economic slowdown had led to lower tax revenues.

However, from FY 2001 to FY 2006, corporate profits increased 6.9 times, from ¥7.1 trillion to ¥49.0 trillion, but corporate tax revenues only grew 45%, from

¥10.3 trillion to ¥14.9 trillion. Moreover, from FY 2008 to FY 2011, corporate profits surged from 22.1 trillion yen to 36.4 trillion yen, but corporate tax revenues on the contrary declined.

As of FY 2011, the corporate tax rate was 30%, and now it is even lower at 23.2%. At this tax rate, even if corporate profits increase in the future, the growth in tax revenue will be extremely limited, and the peak corporate tax revenue of 19 trillion yen achieved in FY 1989 will only become more distant.

As long as people are alive and the country is alive, it is difficult to reduce spending. The only way to avoid a deficit without reducing spending is to increase tax revenue. It is the same as the life of all of us. We can't live without income. Understanding the need to increase tax revenue, we accepted the introduction of the consumption tax.

However, as soon as the consumption tax was introduced, the country's tax revenue began to decline. One reason was that the consumption tax led to an economic slowdown. The other reason was that the government cut taxes on everything except the consumption tax. Isn't this a bit of a trick? The consumption tax is a tax that is harsh on the poor and kind to the rich. Lowering the corporate tax rate and income tax rate is also friendly to the wealthy. In other words, the Japanese government at that time set up a typical tax system for the jungle law. And that trend is still continuing today.

However, the tax reform resulted in 30 years of stagnation in Japan. While the rest of the world continued to run, only Japan fell asleep. The system was designed to reduce Japan's vitality. So, who benefited from such a tax system of the jungle law?

One thing I'm wondering is: It's the employees who support the companies. It is the general public. Then the question is, has the tax system that disrespects the general public really made the companies stronger? This will be examined in the next section.

22. Gains from lowering the corporate tax rate

Chart 23: Corporate tax rate and economic growth rate (Source: Compiled from National Tax Agency and Cabinet Office data)

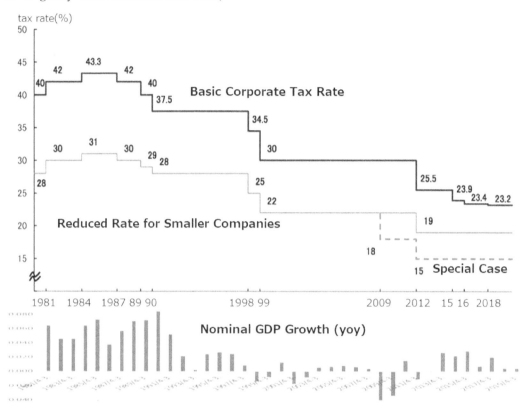

(Note: translated by Arata Yaguchi)

Chart 23 shows the corporate tax rate from FY 1981 to the present, alongside the growth rate of nominal GDP year on year over the same period. The upper line shows the basic corporate tax rate, while the lower line and the dotted line show the corporate tax rate for small and medium enterprises. The bars below show the growth rate of nominal GDP compared to the previous year.

During the period of Japan's rapid economic growth and the bubble economy, the corporate tax rate was higher than it is today. And even with a tax rate of over 40%, Japanese companies were able to achieve rapid economic growth and at one point reached the point where the U.S. was alarmed, saying "Japan, as No. 1." While it is a little uncomfortable to use the past tense of "peaked" for a country that is still ongoing, as a matter of the fact that Japan's economic growth peaked in FY 1997. Japan's tax revenue, the source of the government's power, effectively peaked in FY 1990.

Tax revenue in FY 1990 was 60.1 trillion yen, and in FY 2018 it was 60.4 trillion yen, an increase of 0.3 trillion yen just on a numerical basis. However, when we consider the elements of weakness in the government's economic management in order to achieve this, such as the accumulated budget deficit and public debt, the BOJ's huge money supply and negative interest rate policy, the government's source of power in FY 2018 can never be considered to have surpassed its FY 1990 peak.

From a macroeconomic perspective, tax cuts are an economic stimulus. However, Chart 23 shows that there is even a positive correlation between the corporate tax rate and the economic growth rate. In other words, as tax rates are lowered, the economy worsens. It is unlikely that tax cuts will worsen the economy. If it worsened, there were other factors that made it worse. In the case of Japan, there is a high possibility that the consumption tax, as shown in Chart 02, is a deteriorating factor.

What is the goal of tax reform? Essentially, it is to make the country richer. Economic growth enriches the country. Increased tax revenue enriches the government. Japan's combination of the consumption tax hikes and the corporate tax cuts has stopped both economic growth and tax revenue growth. In other words, it has destroyed the country.

Just as there were plausible explanations for the introduction and increase of the consumption tax, various reasons have been mentioned for lowering the corporate tax rate, such as encouraging companies to become more competitive. However, the competitiveness of Japanese companies, which has been called "Japan's politics is second-rate, but its economy is first-rate," has been declining year by year along with the decline in the corporate tax rate.

For example, in 1989, Japanese companies accounted for 14 of the top 20 companies in the world market capitalization rankings. Now, however, there are none. The TOPIX, which reflects the market capitalization of all stocks on the First Section of the Tokyo Stock Exchange, reached a high of 2884.80 yen in 1989, but the closing price at the end of September 2020 was 1625.49 yen, only 56.3% of its peak.

Incidentally, the U.S. S&P 500 stock price index did not reach $300 at the end of 1989, but rose to nearly $3600 by September 2020.

In addition, in the Global Competitiveness Ranking 2019 released in May 2020 by the International Institute for Management Development in Switzerland, Japan has dropped to 30th place from 25th place the previous year, its lowest ranking ever. Japan's position as the world's No. 1 economy in 1989 is now in the distant past. Not to mention the sharp decline in the number of companies with the highest credit rating, such as triple-A.

The fact that there is a positive correlation between the decline in corporate tax rates and the decline in corporate competitiveness does not necessarily mean that companies have lost their ambition and fighting spirit, as they have been pampered by corporate tax cuts. Mindset can change quickly by external factors. I believe that the main factor that has stopped Japan's economic growth is the introduction of the consumption tax. As I will explain later, it is difficult to even maintain a profit if the consumption tax should be deducted from sales when sales are not growing.

The tax reform that gave preferential treatment to corporations at the expense of the general public, that was the combination of the lowering of the corporate tax rate and the introduction of the consumption tax, resulted not only in a decrease in corporate tax revenue but also in a decline in the competitiveness of corporations.

23. Number of companies with deficits also increased rapidly

Chart 24: Changes in the number of corporations and percentage of loss-making corporations (Source: National Tax Agency data with consumption tax rates written in)

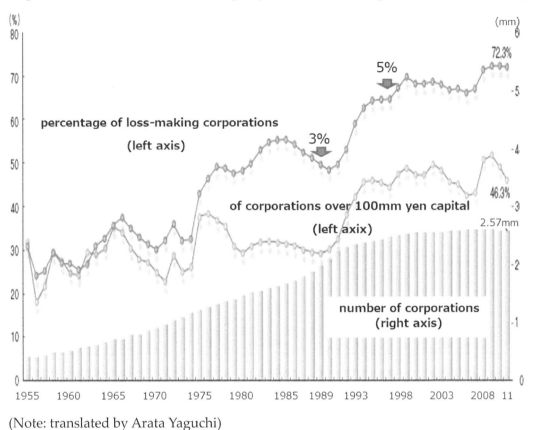

(Note: translated by Arata Yaguchi)

Chart 24 shows the trend in loss-making corporations from 1955 to 2011. A loss-making corporation is a corporation that has a deficit and does not pay taxes. The upper line shows the ratio of loss-making corporations to all corporations. The lower line shows the percentage of loss-making corporations with large capital to all corporations. The bars show the total number of corporations.

After the introduction of the consumption tax, the number of loss-making companies also increased rapidly. The bars at the bottom of the previous Chart 23 show that the Japanese economy slowed down in the year following the introduction of the 3% consumption tax in FY 1989. From FY 1997, when the tax rate was raised to 5%, the economy experienced negative growth. The economic slowdown compared to such negative growth may seem like "only" a slowdown because the comparison is too harsh. However, the number of companies with deficits increased rapidly from FY 1990.

The ratio of loss-making corporations to the total number of corporations, as seen in Chart 24, began to rise sharply in the year following the introduction of the 3% consumption tax in FY 1989. After the tax rate was raised to 5% in FY 1997, the number of corporations with deficits rose further, to over 72% in the three years from FY 2009 to FY 2011. This means that more than 70% of Japanese corporations were in the red.

It should be worth noting that the increase in the number of loss-making corporations is consistent with the slowdown in nominal GDP growth and negative growth, although there are some corporations that dare to run deficits to avoid taxes and others that use various methods to reduce taxes.

Here again, there is no reason to believe that the reduction in the corporate tax rate led to an increase in the number of loss-making corporations, and it is reasonable to assume that the main factor was the economic downturn caused by the introduction of the consumption tax.

This shows that the popular understanding of the consumption tax as being harsh on the general public and lenient on corporations is missing the point, and that it has been very harsh not only on the general public, but also on most corporations. There have been many representatives of business organizations who have been in favor of the consumption tax hike, but what have they seen so far?

On the other hand, Abenomics' negative interest rate policy, the supply of funds exceeding the size of the economy, and the central bank's shareholding in private companies reduced the ratio of deficient corporations, falling to

62.1% in FY 2018. In addition, FY 2017 and FY 2018 were the two consecutive years in which sales and profits of Japanese corporations reached record highs, and tax revenues increased accordingly.

Nevertheless, all of the above policies of Abenomics can be said to have helped corporations at the expense of the general public, and as mentioned above, they have left a number of big problems for the next generation.

24. Consumption tax is deducted from sales

Chart 25: Profit and loss statement

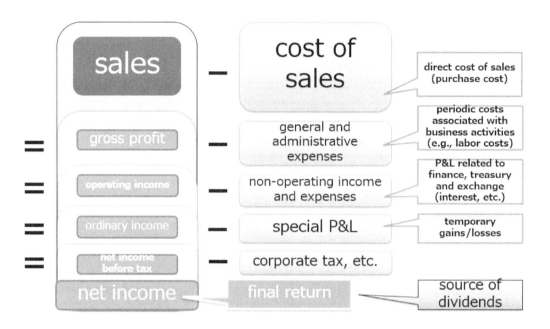

Chart 25 was created to illustrate the profit and loss statement. By subtracting from sales, we arrive at the final return, which is the source of dividends. In the "callout" on the right is the explanation of the subtracting factors.

Subtracting the cost of sales from a company's sales revenue yields gross profit. Subtracting general and administrative expenses from gross profit yields operating income. When non-operating income is added to or subtracted from operating income, and costs are subtracted, ordinary income is obtained. Adding or subtracting special gains and losses from ordinary income yields income before taxes. Subtracting corporate income tax and other taxes from this results in net income, which is to be used as the final return to fund dividends.

Risk and return are two sides of the same coin. From the government's point of view, the consumption tax, which is a stable source of revenue regardless of economic fluctuations, can be taken away even if the economy worsens, but it is like a feudal era tribute that is mercilessly collected even if the income of ordinary people declines and the profits of companies decline. On the other hand, even if the economy improves and income and profits increase, there is no significant increase in tax revenue. In other words, the consumption tax is a low and stable source of revenue.

On the other hand, consumption tax is known to be a tax system that is kind to the rich and harsh to the poor because it taxes the general public uniformly regardless of their income level. It also seems to be understood as being lenient to corporations, but in the previous Chart 24 it was known to be a factor in business deterioration. The reason for this is that the consumption tax is a tax that the government deducts from sales. In other words, while the corporate tax is levied on the last fruits of business activities, the consumption tax is collected on sales, a stage where neither costs nor profits are yet known.

The consumption tax will be a detrimental factor to the economy by squeezing consumer spending. With such sluggish growth of the consumption (= sales) pie, companies will have to pay the consumption tax from their sales. Let's take a look at what this means from a company's profit and loss statement.

The "three-sided equivalence principle" of Gross National Product (GDP) states that the value added accumulated for each sector in which it is created, the value added accumulated from the distributional side such as wages and profits (production side), and the value added from the expenditure on final products such as consumption and capital investment (expenditure side) are always equal. This means that the size and growth rate of the economy can be seen from either the production or consumption side.

Similarly, the expenditures we make are sales on the part of the companies, and the consumption tax we pay will be paid by the companies to the government. The company's sales are bulked up by the consumption tax that will partly disappear in the following year.

Gross profit is calculated by subtracting the cost of sales from sales, but this cost of sales is also subject to the consumption tax. In other words, profits decrease by the amount of cost increase. All this economic activity from that point to net income before taxes is subject to the consumption tax, which pressures profits as a cost.

If costs rise when there is no increase in revenue, profits will decrease. In order to escape a decrease in profit, cost reduction will be carried out. They will cut labor costs, reduce capital expenditures, and cut research and development expenses. This was generally what companies that had to pay the consumption tax was doing as the economy had shrunk since FY 1997. The situation has been even more miserable for subcontractors and sub-subcontractors, since they were considered to be costs of the upper companies.

I started my career at the Tokyo branch of a British company, and then worked for a Japanese company, American companies, and a Swiss company. I know a lot of good and bad things about Japanese companies, so I don't feel like defending them too much. However, I have also keenly felt the problems of foreign companies.

It has been said that the decline in the competitiveness of Japanese companies is due to the fact that they have not changed their old structure, but it is true that they were even said to be number one, even if only temporarily, because of that old structure. However, from the time of the introduction of the consumption tax, the economy suddenly went into a downturn and many companies began to lose money (as Chart 24 shows). Then, people started to say that the old way of doing things was wrong.

The consumption tax, while stable at a low level, is like charging 10 percent at the seed and seedling stage, unable to wait for the fall harvest. This will cause production to stagnate and tax revenue to decline because the source of the harvest has been taken away. It is like a body blow to the economy, hurting it to the core.

25. Income tax

Table 03: Income tax quick calculation table (Source: National Tax Agency, 2015 and later)

Income tax quick calculation table

Amount of taxable income	Rate	Deduction amount
1,000 ～ 1,949,000 yen	5%	¥ 0円
1,950,000 ～ 3,299,000 yen	10%	¥ 97,500円
3,300,000 ～ 6,949,000 yen	20%	¥ 427,500円
6,950,000 ～ 8,999,000 yen	23%	¥ 636,000円
9,000,000 ～ 17,999,000 yen	33%	¥ 1,536,000円
18,000,000 ～ 39,999,000 yen	40%	¥ 2,796,000円
over 40,000,000	45%	¥ 4,796,000円

(Note: translated by Arata Yaguchi)

Table 03 is a quick calculation table of income tax on the National Tax Agency's website, and it shows a progressive taxation system in which the tax rate increases as the amount of taxable income increases. The point to note here is that the income covered is the taxable income, not the annual income. Taxable income is defined as annual income minus various deductions. In addition to income tax, individual resident tax, pension insurance premiums, health insurance premiums, nursing care insurance premiums, and unemployment insurance premiums are also deducted from annual income.

History has shown that there are ups and downs in the economic activities of any country. Most people who have lived long enough may realize that there are good times and bad times in life. Many people can relate to the fact that the same 1,000 yen or 10,000 yen weighs differently in good times and in hard times. However, the consumption tax is a tax that is deducted from many economic activities of the Japanese people, no matter what the situation is.

Just think of the interest payment on a loan. Interest payments when you are in good shape may be nothing. However, when there are sudden expenses due to illness, injury, wedding, funeral, etc., or when there is no bonus, for example, the interest payment as usual becomes difficult. The social security system is supported by the workers of the general public, who individually have a wide range of circumstances. With this in mind, we can see that the consumption tax is not an essential tax, but a cold-blooded bad tax.

When times are tough, even a 1% interest rate is painful, but on the other hand, when things are going well, even a 50% interest rate is neither painful nor itchy. The world is made up of a system where things come from plentiful to scarce. To try to take something from those who have virtually nothing is not only difficult, but also destabilizes society and makes the world unsustainable.

The income tax is a tax that is taken from those who are in good financial shape, or when someone happens to be in good shape. Incidentally, the corporate tax is the corporate version of the income tax, but we already know that the tax rate has been changed to a rate that does not make so much revenue even when things are going well.

The current income tax system is a progressive taxation with seven brackets ranging from a minimum tax rate of 5% (income of 1,000 yen to 1,499,000 yen: no deduction) to a maximum tax rate of 45% (income of 40 million yen or more: deduction of 4,796,000 yen).

The typical amount of money left on hand after taxes, deductions, social insurance premiums from annual income is about 2.4 million yen for 3 million yen, about 3.9 million yen for 5 million yen, about 5.6 million yen for 7.5 million yen, about 7.1 million yen for 10 million yen, about 12.7 million yen for 20 million yen, about 1,750 yen for 30 million yen, and about 49 million yen for 100 million yen.

What this shows is that as income increases, the amount of money left over becomes large enough so that there is no problem with it being taken. I say "no problem" because the cost of essential housing, cars, clothing, food, etc. is not much different for everyone. There is a limit to how much you can spend, even if it is quite extravagant.

In light of the fact that high income ultimately comes from society, wouldn't it make "sense" to say that social security funding should be fulfilled by increasing the progressive income tax rate? It's rather good to go on a spree with easy money. It is better for the economy than just saving. But if you take away the "surplus income" through income tax and use it to fund social security, the money will come to more desperate places.

26. Individual resident tax

Chart 26: Progressive income taxation (Source: written in Ministry of Finance data)

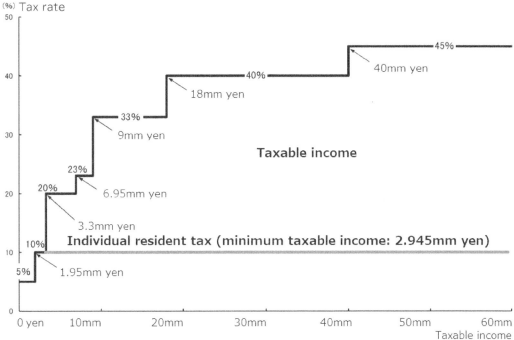

(Note: translated by Arata Yaguchi)

Chart 26 shows a graph of the progressive income tax rates seen in Table 03, with the individual resident tax added. The horizontal axis is the taxable income, and the vertical axis is the income tax rate. It can be seen that as the taxable income increases, the tax rate increases. On the other hand, the individual resident tax is levied at a flat rate of 10% regardless of income (minimum taxable income: 2,945,000 yen).

What we notice here is that in addition to the income tax, the individual resident tax is levied at a flat rate of 10%. Because of this, high-income earners lament that more than half of their income is taken away by taxes. However, the high-income earners still have a lot of money left over, but what about the middle- and low-income earners? Looking at it this way, the combined tax rate for those with a taxable income of 3.3 million yen would be as high as

30%, greatly undermining the effect of progressive taxation.

Let us now look back again at Chart 01, which we mentioned at the beginning of this chapter, and see that from FY 1990 the budget deficit widened as the tax revenues began to decline. This means that the tax revenues had been growing steadily until FY 1989, when the consumption tax was introduced. However, as mentioned above, after peaking at 60.1 trillion yen in FY 1990, Japan's tax revenue suddenly began to decline.

Chart 01: Consumption tax and total tax revenue (Source: Ministry of Finance with arrows consumption tax rates inserted)

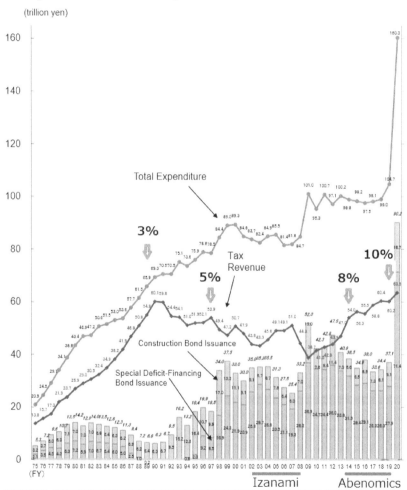

By looking back at Chart 02, we also see the relation between economic growth and total tax revenue, and the breakdown of the tax revenue. Economic growth began to decelerate in FY 1990, the year after the consumption tax was introduced. And from FY 1997, when the consumption tax was raised to 5%, economic growth became negative, and it will have to wait until Abenomics in FY 2013 to return to decent positive growth.

Abenomics is a series of forbidden economic policies, including the supply of funds that exceed the size of the economy, fiscal financing, negative interest rate policies, and stock purchases by the central bank. I say "forbidden" because, in addition to its marginal monetary policies, it has postponed a great deal of risk for future generations by ruining the function of the government bond market, severely undermining the profitability of bank lending operations, increasing the country's credit risk, and making the central bank the largest shareholder of Japanese corporations.

And in FY 2018, when the effects of Abenomics were at their maximum, the tax revenues reached 60.4 trillion yen. But after the consumption tax rate hike, the vulnerable economy that has relied on inbound tourism and the counter-Corona measures that halted economic activity pushed the tax revenue to start to decline. In other words, Abenomics has just left a tremendous risk for future generations and has spit out all of its effects as far as macroeconomic and tax revenues are concerned.

Chart 02: Tax revenue and nominal GDP growth (Source: Compiled from data of the Ministry of Finance and the Cabinet Office)

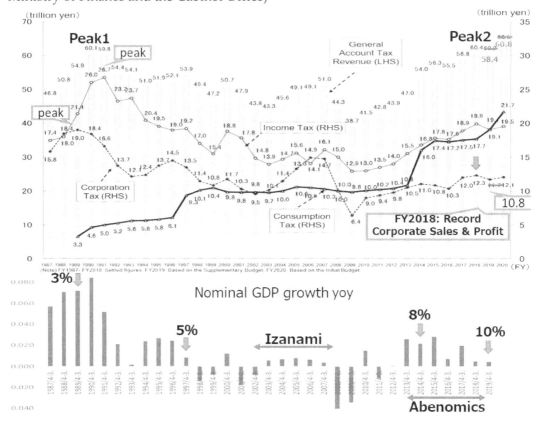

Chart 02 shows that corporate tax revenue peaked in FY 1989 when the consumption tax was introduced. Total tax revenue peaked in FY 1990. The income tax revenue peaked in FY 1991. It must be difficult to keep spending down from the previous year, but as long as tax revenues were growing, the budget deficit would not have continued to balloon.

27. Lies and truths of "One For All, All For One"

Chart 27: Trends in the progressivity of income tax and individual resident tax (Source: Ministry of Finance)

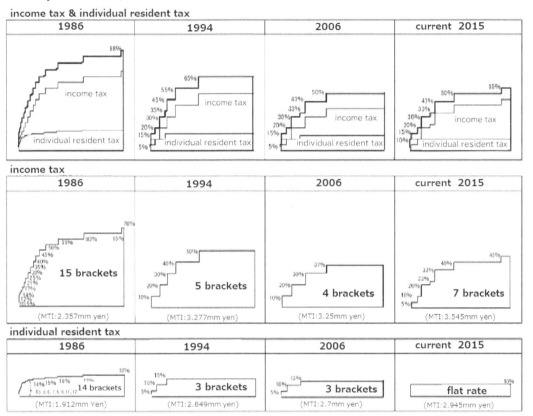

*MTI: minimum taxable income

(Note: translated by Arata Yaguchi)

Chart 27 shows the trends in income tax and individual resident tax from 1986 to 2015, in order from the top: income tax and individual resident tax combined, income tax only, and individual resident tax only.

I have mentioned above that the corporate tax has become a source of revenue that can no longer be expected to grow significantly because the corporate tax rate has been continually lowered to that extent. On the other hand, the consumption tax is a stable source of revenue, so it is mercilessly withheld in times of economic recession, but even in periods of economic expansion, no significant growth is expected. Then, what about the income tax? Let's look at the tax rate at the time of the increase in tax revenue seen on the left side of the previous Chart 01 and 02 in Chart 27.

The income tax around 1986, seen on the far left of Chart 27, was a progressive tax with 15 brackets. And since the individual resident tax was also progressive with 14 brackets, the highest tax rate both combined was as high as 88%. In other words, when Japan was shining, income tax was taken as much as possible from those who could afford it. Also, there was no consumption tax, so they did not overreach where they could not. Even so, the economy was expanding, businesses were strong, personal income was increasing, and the budget balance was almost balanced. On the other hand, the right side shows the current situation, and as mentioned above, the highest tax rate is 55%.

So, with income tax at a high rate of 88%, were the high-income earners of the time unhappy? For example, a taxable annual income of 100 million yen would leave 12 million yen on hand; 200 million yen would leave 24 million yen; and 1 billion yen would leave 120 million yen. Does this make it any less incentive?

At that time, the Japanese people achieved rapid economic growth without losing their sense of motivation, and even reached the bubble economy. Many people were so buoyant that they played around. Even if managers increased their own compensation, nearly 90% would be taken by taxes, so they invested in equipment, raised labor costs, and as if it was "One For All, All For One," the entire company was able to go about its business as a united team. The unemployment rate, shown in Chart 09 above, was also low at around 2%, and the trend in employment status shown in the previous Chart 10 shows that more than 80% of the employees were in regular and stable employment. In order to foster a mindset of serving the team, it is vital to create a more equal environment.

Before 1989, Japanese companies were strong because labor and management were more equal. And the progressive income tax system encouraged this. In the current environment, where the percentage of non-regular employees is high and management can bring in compensation that is many times, dozens of times, or in the U.S. style, hundreds of times higher than the average employee, "One For All, All For One" sounds like a convenient call for management.

According to a study by Toyo Keizai, Takeda's average executive compensation in FY 2019 was more than 55 times the average annual employee salary, the highest multiple in Japan. At the same time, the company made a large number of layoffs in the same year. In addition, the average compensation received in 2018 by CEOs of 500 major U.S. companies was 287 times that of ordinary employees, according to American Federation of Labor–Congress of Industrial Organizations.

28. Downgrade

Chart 28：Trends in Japanese Government Bond ratings by major rating agencies (Source: Ministry of Finance)

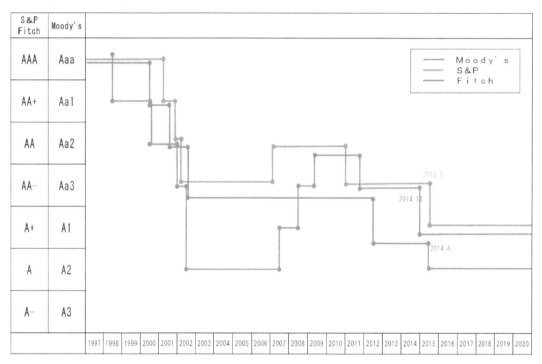

Chart 28 shows the credit ratings of Japanese government bonds by the world's major rating agencies, Moody's, S&P and Fitch, from 1997 to 2020. The upper line on the far left is S&P, the lower one is Fitch, and the one starting in the middle is the rating by Moody's.

For at least a decade, Japanese government bonds had been rated triple-A by all three rating agencies, the highest possible rating. Since 1999, the rating has been downgraded by Moody's, Fitch, and S&P, one after another. This shows that Japan's ability to repay its debt has been continuously downgraded.

A credit rating is a tiered rating of an issuer's ability to successfully repay the principal and interest on its debt.

While the Japanese government's outstanding debt continues to grow, it has not seen the growth in tax revenues that can be a promise to repay. In this sense, of the three rating agencies, Fitch rating, which has been consistently downgraded, seems to best reflect the fundamentals of the Japanese government. On the other hand, according to Moody's, the rating of Japanese government bonds rose temporarily and is still higher than the worst period, but what exactly does this rating agency see in the Japanese government's financial situation and what does it expect?

Anyhow, do you know what to do when you are driving in a strange place and get lost? Nowadays, you would say, "Just follow the GPS, I'll never go the wrong way because I have GPS." This means that you are leaving risk management to the GPS. For example, if guided by hackers, you could even be kidnapped.

The car I bought in 1990 had a GPS, but it was still accurate enough to drive over the ocean from time to time. Earlier cars didn't have GPS, and so I had to check the road map and memorize the key crossroads. When you make a wrong turn, the " golden rule" is to go back to the place where you think you made the mistake. Guessing that you should be able to get to the original destination by going this way or another can be fatal in a foreign country.

Japan took a wrong turn when the consumption tax was introduced combining with the income tax cuts and the corporate tax cuts. To put it simply, after 1989, Japan became a completely different country. The first thing that happened immediately was a decline in tax revenue, followed by negative growth. And while the consumption tax and its rate hike were kept sacrosanct, as the government has taken other measures to combat negative growth, disinflation, budget deficit and so on, the distortions became apparent everywhere, as I have mentioned.

For example, from FY 1990 to FY 2009, the tax revenues basically declined steadily. The expenditures, however, continued to grow until FY 2000, resulting in a sharp increase in the budget deficit. Therefore, the spending cuts began in FY 2001, but as we will see later, Japan's total population peaked in 2008, so the government was forced to reduce spending even as the population grew. Since spending due to corruption and waste has not been easily reduced unfortunately, the government has cut even essential items.

In the case of a company, it would be like increasing the number of new employees even though both sales and profits are declining, and cutting personnel expenses, capital investment, and R&D expenses while not cutting executive compensation or executive expenses. In general, this is what many companies have done. Basically, this has been the trend since FY 1997. This can inevitably lead to a decline in the competitiveness of companies.

In addition, because the government responded to the economic slowdown by cutting the interest rates, Japan's policy rate hit 0.51% in March 1997 and has remained below 0.50% since then. This basically means that there is no longer any risk-free investment vehicle. A few years would be fine, but 20+ years on the same path of extreme difficulty is too long. In this way, the business model that relies on interest income has become more like a structural recession.

To top it all off, there is the negative interest rate policy. Banks and life insurers have been selling their stock holdings for more than a decade to adjust their accounting figures. The Bank of Japan stated the following in its verification report of the negative interest rate policy issued on September 5, 2016.

(Partial quote below, end at URL)

4. Effects and Impact of Negative Interest Rates

(Impact on the financial intermediary function)

In general, financial institutions have a basic structure of "short-term funding and long-term investment," and since deposit interest rates, the main means of funding, are unlikely to be negative, a decline in the level of interest rates across the yield curve or a decrease in the difference between short-term and long-term interest rates will lead to a contraction in the loan-deposit margin, which will have a negative impact on earnings.

In particular, in the case of Japan, the impact of negative interest rates on the earnings of financial institutions is expected to be relatively large because the balance of deposits greatly exceeds the balance of loans, and the loan-deposit margin is already at an extremely low level due to the long period of competition among financial institutions.

In addition, after the introduction of negative interest rates, the levels of long-term interest rates and ultra-long-term interest rates have fallen sharply, and under these circumstances, investment yields on insurance and pensions have been expected to fall, and some savings-type products were forced to be suspended. Some companies have seen an increase in their retirement benefit obligations based on discounted present value, which has been a factor in lower profits.

(Note: translated by Arata Yaguchi)

Reference: "Comprehensive Review" of Monetary Accommodation Policy
http://www.boj.or.jp/announcements/press/koen_2016/data/ko160905a1.pdf

In other words, the Bank of Japan itself has clearly stated the negative impact of the negative interest rate policy on financial institutions. At the same time, the Financial Services Agency estimated that "more than 60% of regional banks would go into the red in their core business" due to the negative interest rate policy.

What they reveal is that banks have become a structurally depressed industry as a result of the Bank of Japan's monetary policy. And the government authorities were well aware of this.

Then-Prime Minister Yoshihide Suga, who inherited Abenomics, was reported to have said that the regional banks are not taking their jobs seriously and that they should use their own wisdom to create jobs and employment in rural areas, and that it would be difficult to save banks that do not make such efforts. This is like saying that banks should somehow make money outside of the "financial intermediary function". It means that traditional banking is no longer needed.

He says he is not going to "save the banks," but they wouldn't have been cornered if not for the policies of the authorities. To me, they look like they are being forced to surrender their castles after years of lockdown. The reason why the regional banks appear to be "not serious" is because some of them are not fighting back against the government's attacks, but are just hunkering down and eating their own assets.

As will be discussed later, the Japanese government has the world's highest debt to GDP ratio. And Japanese government's net debt to GDP ratio is also the highest among the countries surveyed. Yet, it still maintains an investment grade rating of single-A. The reasons for this will also be explained later.

29. Ballooning public debt

Chart 29: The scale of outstanding debt is unprecedented (Source: Ministry of Finance)

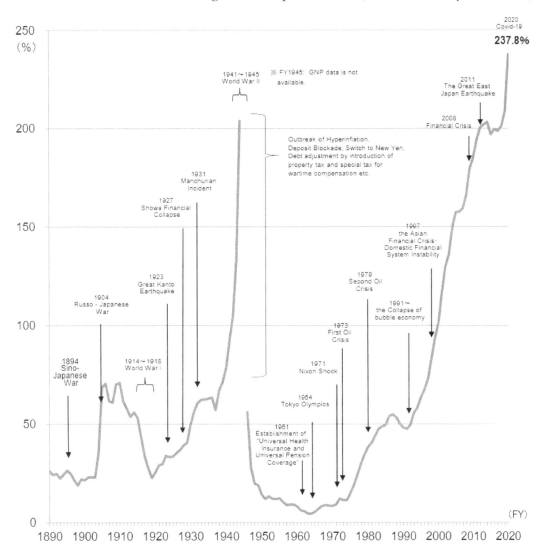

Chart 29 shows the ratio of Japan's outstanding public debt to GDP from FY 1890 to FY 2020 on the Ministry of Finance's website. They have written down the events that are supposed to have a significant impact on the outstanding debt.

I don't think Japan's GDP was that large before World War II, but even so, the outstanding public debt was far below GDP even during the Sino-Japanese War, Russo-Japanese War, Showa Financial Depression and Manchurian Incident. In World War II, it skyrocketed to over 200% of GDP and eventually led to the denomination of currency devaluation. I was told by my mother and my aunts what hardship Japanese people had during this period.

Even after the war, there was the Nixon shock that led to the shift to a floating exchange rate system for currencies, and the oil shock, but until the bubble period, the debt was capped at just over 50% of GDP. However, as mentioned above, with tax revenues peaking in 1990, there has been virtually no way to prevent the expansion of debt.

In other words, after 1989, Japan became a completely different country. Unfortunately, the government continued to hike the consumption tax as if it were the only thing on its mind, even though it was unable to revive the economy or increase tax revenue. It is obvious to everyone that we have taken a wrong turn, but only the drivers and their cronies are saying, "This is fine. We have to ask the people for raising the consumption tax," and they have continued on the same path. As a result, the accumulated budget deficit continued to swell, and the outstanding public debt that was used to finance it reached an unprecedented scale, as seen in Chart 29.

If anyone looks at Chart 29 and thinks that it is unavoidable because there was the Lehman Shock or the Great East Japan Earthquake, they do not understand risk management at all. Both good and bad things can happen in the world. Risk management is based on the premise that you never know what will happen. That is why we need economic growth and increased tax revenue. Nuclear power plants caused a lot of damage in the Great East Japan Earthquake, but this was also a problem of risk management.

We can see from Chart 29 that the angle of increase becomes sharper from around 1990. The rightmost figure is for 2020, but it is actually the one of a couple of years ago, and even then, the angle has already become even steeper, on par with the angle on the eve of World War II. And, as we have seen so far, there is no prospect of paying off this debt with the current tax system.

As a matter of fact, Japan is not the only country that has been rapidly increasing its public debt even before the Corona pandemic. Nevertheless, those countries have done something about it, as we will see in the next section.

30. Greece and Italy have had austerity measures

Chart 30: Japan's Public Debt to GDP Ratio (Source: OECD, 2015)

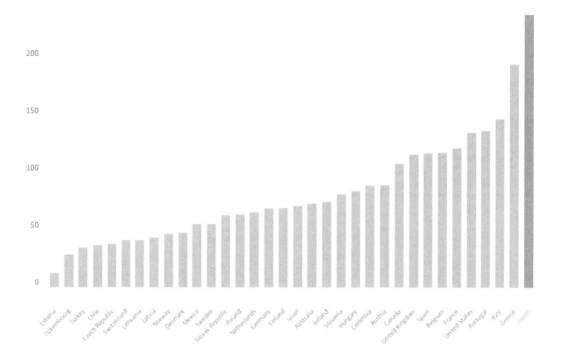

Chart 30 shows a comparison of public debt as a percentage of GDP for OECD countries as of 2015. The dark bar on the far right is that of Japan, with only one country exceeding 200%. You also know that Japan's public debt has continued to increase since then, while the size of the economy, which was stopped by the counter-Corona measures, has shrunk. In other words, this dark bar should have grown further up as the numerator got bigger and the denominator got smaller.

Some of you may remember that Greece, the country to the left of Japan, has adopted an intense austerity policy and many civil servants were among the rapidly growing number of unemployed.

Italy, Greece's neighbor to the left and has a much smaller public debt as a percentage of GDP than Japan, held a referendum in September 2020 on reducing the number of parliament members. The vote in favor of the reduction was 69.64%, more than double the 30.36% who voted against. As a result, the number of seats in the Lower House reduced from 630 to 400, and the number of seats in the Upper House from 315 to 200, for an overall reduction of nearly 40%.

What are Japan's politicians and bureaucrats, sitting on the largest debt of any country, going to do about it? Japan's civil service staffing capacity will increase for the first time in 42 years. In addition, shortly after the Suga administration took office in September 2020, Toshihiro Nikai, former secretary-general of the Liberal Democratic Party, was said to have instructed the government to start considering the restoration of the Diet members' mutual aid pension, which was abolished in 2006, and the local government members' pension, which was abolished in 2011.

31. Japan is ranked 113th out of 113 countries

Chart 31: International comparison of outstanding debt (Source: Ministry of Finance)

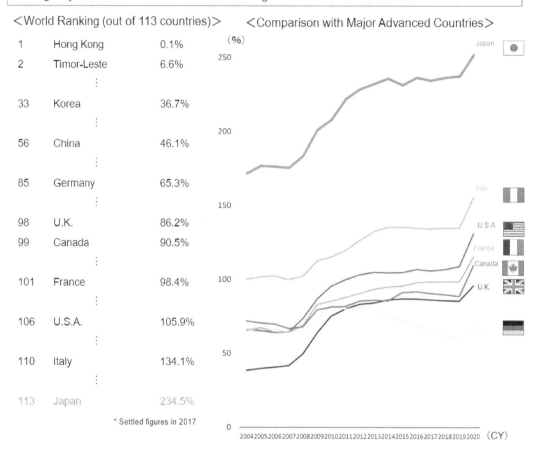

Chart 31 shows an international comparison of the ratio of public debt to GDP on the website of the Ministry of Finance. On the left are the rankings and figures for 2017, and on the right are the public debt-to-GDP ratios of the G7 countries from 2004 to 2020. The upper most line is that of Japan, which is far larger than any other country.

This shows that the ratio of Japan's outstanding public debt to GDP is now over 250%. It is now clear that the figure of 237.8% for the year 2020 in the right side of Chart 29 above is wrong. And it is confirmed wrong when the figure is compared with the OECD chart of 2015 in Chart 30 above.

Chart 31 shows that in 2017, Japan's debt-to-GDP ratio was 234.5%, ranking 113th among 113 countries in the comparative survey. The IMF has predicted that Japan's public debt will be 266% of GDP in 2020, which still seems modest given the rapid increase in debt in the numerator and the decline in GDP in the denominator.

32. How about in terms of net debt outstanding?

Chart 32: International comparison of net debt outstanding (Source: Ministry of Finance)

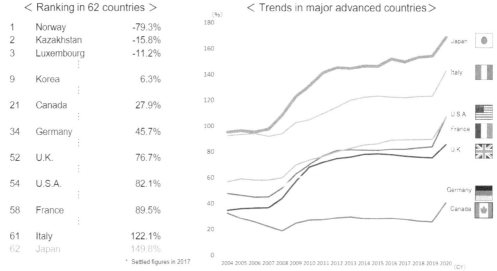

Chart 32 shows an international comparison of the ratio of net debt to GDP, which is the sum of assets and debt, because it is not fair to compare only debt. On the left are the rankings of the 62 countries surveyed and their net debt to GDP ratios. On the right is the trend of the G7 countries from 2004 to 2020. The upper line is for Japan, which again leads the other countries.

Since Japan is a creditor nation, some people believe that there is no problem even if the outstanding public debt is the highest in the world, as seen in the previous Chart 31. However, in terms of net debt, the Japanese government has already reached 150% of GDP in 2017, ranking 62nd out of 62 countries surveyed; the chart on the right, depicting 2020, shows 170%.

It is still 80% lower than the outstanding debt alone, but this offsetting of assets and liabilities is a part of the equation game that cannot necessarily be taken at face value. In other words, the assets are only valuation, while the liabilities are cash equivalents.

Have you ever heard of goodwill? It is the amount of money paid by a buyer over and above the seller's net worth in a corporate acquisition. It is an added premium, and is also considered an asset because there is a buyer. On the other hand, something like a debt of gratitude, expressed as "I owe that person," is not considered a debt.

In other words, payment of outstanding debt requires "cash" to cover the balance, but assets are "valuation gains" that become actual cash when there is a buyer. That's why there are cases where the company defaults on its debt even if its net worth is positive. It doesn't matter how many of Maestro's highly rated "pie in the sky" you have, it won't necessarily help you in times of emergency.

Japan is a creditor nation, but the Japanese government is a net debtor government. This means that it is the private sector in Japan that holds the assets. Nevertheless, the reason why the net debt of the Japanese government in Chart 32 is less than that of the public debt in Chart 31 is that the Japanese government itself has some assets. This is probably why the major rating agencies have evaluated it and given it a single A investment grade rating, as mentioned above.

Chart 32 provides an explanation of such financial assets held by the government. That is the assets "such as pension reserves consisting of pension premiums" from the people. What is the creditor nation? Why is it safe? Japan' government is just full of debt and all the assets they think of theirs belong to the people. The government relies on the people.

Incidentally, Japan's public pension system has a reserve fund that can cover benefits for about four years. This is because Japan's public pension system is compulsory, and all adults, including students, start accumulating funds when they turn 20. In comparison, the U.S. has about three years, the U.K. about four months, Germany about two months, and France almost nothing. Even with the addition of these assets, the Japanese government has more debt than it has assets, ranking 62nd out of 62 countries in terms of net debt.

The same can be said for Japan's debt, which is often said to be "okay because it is not foreign currency denominated debt." Argentina and Lebanon, which have far less debt than Japan, defaulted on their debt in the summer of 2020. If a country defaults on its debt, creditor nations and international organizations will demand it doing what Greece and Italy did. The reason why these two countries defaulted, even though they had less debt was, because their debt was denominated in foreign currencies.

However, since most of the Japanese government bonds are digested in Japan, they say "it's okay". This is like saying that since the buyers (lenders) are the people's assets, such as pensions, life insurance, and bank deposits, the government can confiscate them at any time. In fact, after World War II, the government not only effectively defaulted on the people's JGB assets, but also raised taxes to take away their assets after closing their bank accounts.

What this shows is that the government is dependent on the people. And the Japanese government is the most dependent on the people in the world. You cannot rely on the government. The government relies on you. The government's support and campaigns as counter-Corona measures are simply the government's discretionary allocation of funds that you have given or will give in some form.

We should not expect too much from the government. No, we can expect nothing from it. As I will explain later, Japan's social security system is on the verge of collapse. This is because the government is relying on the people's assets and accumulating debt without the means to repay it.

Therefore, as one of the means of self-reliance that anyone can take on their own, I am providing investment education using the knowledge, experience, and expertise I have gained over the years. As a dealer, I traded the three major instruments of foreign exchange, bonds, and stocks, and worked in the three major markets of Tokyo, New York, and London. I hope that many Japanese people will have the means to become financially independent, and that by looking at things like the consumption tax with an investor's eye, and by leading the way to its abolition, Japan will regain its old glory.

Chapter 2: The Widening Wealth Gap Created

33. The widening gap between the rich and the poor created

On October 7, 2020, two symbolic articles about the global wealth gap appeared in the U.S. media. The first one was the following article from the Wall Street Journal. Only the beginning of the article is to be quoted here.

"The Coronavirus pandemic has thrown between 88 million and 114 million people into extreme poverty, according to the World Bank's biennial estimates of global poverty.

The reversal is by far the largest increase in extreme poverty going back to 1990 when the data begin, and marks an end to a streak of more than two decades of declines in the number of the extremely impoverished, which the World Bank defines as living on less than $1.90 a day, or about $700 a year.

The World Bank now estimates a total of between 703 million and 729 million people are in extreme poverty, and that the number could rise further in 2021."

Reference: Coronavirus Has Thrown Around 100 Million People Into Extreme Poverty, World Bank Estimates
https://www.wsj.com/articles/coronavirus-has-thrown-around-100-million-people-into-extreme-poverty-world-bank-estimates-11602086400

The other one was the following article from CNBC. Let me quote only the beginning of the article, this one as well.

"Billionaire wealth jumped by more than a quarter during the height of the Coronavirus crisis, according to new research, with a rally in stock markets helping the wealth of the world's richest surpass the $10 trillion mark for the first time.
The "Riding the storm" study, published on Wednesday by Swiss bank UBS and

accounting firm PwC, found that global billionaire wealth climbed to $10.2 trillion between April and July this year, up from $8 trillion at the start of April.

That reflected an increase in wealth of 27.5% and exceeded the previous peak of $8.9 trillion recorded at the end of 2017. The number of billionaires worldwide also reached a new high of 2,189, compared to the previous record of 2,158 in 2017."

Reference: Total billionaire wealth surges to record high of $10.2 trillion during coronavirus crisis, research says
https://www.cnbc.com/2020/10/07/coronavirus-billionaire-wealth-hits-record-high-of-10point2-trillion.html

The first news was the first shift to the expansion of the extremely poor in more than 20 years, and the second news was that the number of billionaires has become the largest ever in terms of both number and assets.

As a countermeasure against covid-19, the Japanese government has asked people to refrain from all activities in their daily lives, including the suspension of some economic activities. I suspect that the actual damage caused by these measures, including health damage, is greater than the damage caused by the virus itself. This is because short-term, hard-line measures are not only economically burdensome but may also induce various sorts of fatigue. There is no doubt that covid-19 is a troublesome epidemic, that is why we need to take long-term measures that can be affordable for years.

Nevertheless, the problem that this chapter addresses is the fact that this has led to a widening gap. I take the iconic U.S. case as example, sales in some industries dropped by more than 90 percent year over year as business activity was halted by the counter-Corona measures. Companies laid off many workers, either permanently or temporarily, and at one point the number of people receiving unemployment benefits reached 25.073 million.

The unemployed were at home when they saw the news that the government had decided to support those companies. And the stock prices soared. The owners of the companies became billionaires, while the CEOs, whose compensation was linked to the stock price, found out that they had been paid huge sums of money.

This is not the first time this has happened. These things have happened repeatedly whenever CEOs of US companies resign due to poor performance or scandals.

And the widening gap between the rich and the poor is not limited to the United States. According to Oxford Economics, for example, New York City is the city with the largest number of wealthy people in the world with a net worth of $30 million or more. Next is Hong Kong. Tokyo is the third, with nearly 8,000 residents. Paris and London have fewer than 5,000 people. Japan has dropped down the ranks in terms of global country rankings, corporate competitiveness, and individual income levels, but it is still one of the top-ranked countries in terms of the number of wealthy people.

One of the main themes of the World Economic Forum (Davos) over the past several years has always been the issue of wealth disparity. The world's population is now approaching 7.7 billion, and only six or seven billionaires own as much wealth as the bottom half of the population does. If a few billionaires gave all of their wealth to the bottom 3.8 billion people, their wealth would double. Alternatively, the top 1% of high-income earners will own 33% of all financial assets in the US as of 2019, while the bottom 50% will own only 2% combined. If the top 1% gave up 10% of their wealth, the wealth of the bottom 50% would increase by 2.5 times.

This suggests that the widening gap between the rich and the poor is reinforcing the global deflationary trend: if 100 million people buy a car every 10 years, 10 million cars will be sold every year. On the other hand, if 10 wealthy people buy 100 cars every year, it will only amount to 1,000 cars. The world's central banks are supplying money on an unprecedented scale, but much of it is being sucked into the vaults of the wealthy.

However, even they do not seem to be enjoying such wealth too much: Tesla founder Mr. Elon Musk, who became the world's richest man at least temporarily after the stock market rally in 2021, reportedly sold his previous home and borrowed money to pay for living expenses in 2019 when Tesla stock was slumping. He said this was because he feared that selling his own holdings would have him out of control of the company. Nevertheless, in October 2020, he said on Twitter that the company had been in financial trouble from mid-2017 to mid-2019 and was about a month away from bankruptcy.

A handful of these billionaires, including Microsoft founder Mr. Bill Gates, are proposing to raise income taxes on the wealthy. It's not just because they're modest, but also because too much wealth is now an inconvenience, and the disparity between rich and poor undermines social stability.

Families can no longer live by themselves in their sprawling mansions. Private planes and luxury yachts require the help of others to operate and maintain. Too much wealth means no privacy, and when there are so many people who want to take advantage of it, it's not a bad idea to return to the quiet life of the past with moderate wealth. Although, no one can go back to the days when people were afraid of nothing and only pursued their dreams.

It was "society" that provided them with that wealth in the first place. In order to maintain the stability of the society, why don't they release 90% of the wealth? That way, the lives of the billionaires living in the "society" will be more stable.

There are signs that the trend of lowering income tax rates in the US is reversing. Most people are in favor of raising the income tax rate in 2021. The following is a quote from the beginning of the article on Yahoo Finance, dated

October 8, 2020.

"Yahoo Finance and Harris Poll recently surveyed Americans about taxes and asked if respondents would support an income tax increase in 2021 — which would likely hit them personally — if the additional funds went to either government services or toward paying down the national debt.

Three-quarters of Americans said they're either strongly or somewhat in support of higher income taxes if the funds go toward government services. Additionally, 68% are in favor if the money goes toward paying down the national debt, which currently sits at over $27 trillion and could grow fast in the coming years."

Reference: Most Americans support higher taxes if it's spent on these 2 things
https://finance.yahoo.com/news/most-americans-support-higher-taxes-if-it-goes-to-these-2-things-poll-181050357.html

President Joe Biden has mentioned raising taxes on the wealthy and corporations. Treasury Secretary Janet Yellen also cited American workers relief as her focus and said the U.S. can afford higher corporate tax rate if it coordinates with other countries.

34. The widening wealth gap can be stopped!

Chart 33: Trends in standard VAT rates in various countries (Source: Ministry of Finance)

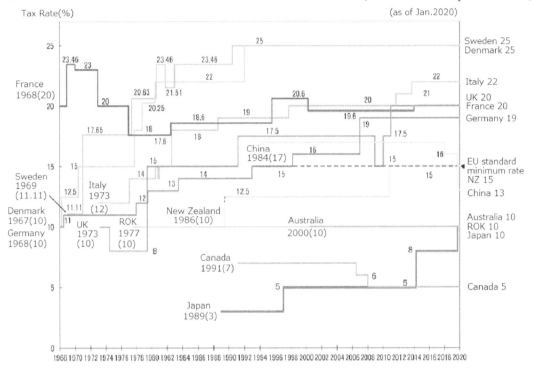

(Note: translated by Arata Yaguchi)

Chart 33 shows the evolution of the consumption tax (value added tax) rates since each country introduced it. This shows that the EU has set a standard tax rate, with a lower limit of 15%. The consumption tax was not in place anywhere before 1966, and if we exclude France, which has had a high tax rate of 20% since its introduction, we can see that in many countries the tax rate has been rising since its introduction there.

Closing the gap between the rich and the poor may possibly be difficult. Because in addition to the traditional inequalities in educational opportunities, recent years have seen platform companies monopolize, control, use, and sell customer information, and dominate financial, delivery, and retail price competition. In addition, the increase in non-regular employment and the tendency of corporate income distribution to favor managers have also contributed to the fixation of inequality.

But improvement is easy. Since the global consumption tax hike (Chart 33), income tax cut (Chart 43 below) and corporate tax cut (Chart 44 below) have contributed to the widening gap between the rich and the poor, we can reverse the trend.

Chart 33 shows that the history of consumption taxes, including value-added tax, is not very old; it was introduced in European countries around 1967. What this shows is that Japan's tax rate is still on the low side. Seeing this, the advocates of higher taxes in Japan have been calling for raising the consumption tax rate to the level of other countries, but no country has ever stopped economic growth like Japan has.

What did globalization mean for Japan? In the 1980s, Japanese companies boasted that they were the most competitive in the world. The trade surplus was so huge that the U.S. pointed to it as a problem. What was being said at the time was that there was nothing in the world that could compete with products developed for the discerning Japanese consumer.

However, while many countries have grown by taking advantage of Japan's technology, Japan's domestic industry has been hollowed out, and economic growth stopped after FY 1997. As domestic consumption stagnated, Japan began to rely on overseas consumers for inbound tourism and special economic zones. If the cause of the stagnation is the strong yen, it is not logical to rely on inbound consumption, which is meant to force people to buy more expensive Japanese products.

This, in turn, suggests that Japan does not need to be so afraid of the globalization crisis, which is currently shaken by the full-scale confrontation between the US and China. This is because the benefits of globalization are limited in light of the fact that Japan's growth stopped in 1997. While the global market has grown, the Japanese economy has shrunk. In dollar terms,

Japan's economy has grown, but this is due to the appreciation of the yen.

This implies that the benefits from the Chinese market were smaller than what Japan lost. A full-scale confrontation between the US and China is also an opportunity if you want to take business away from Chinese companies. In fact, Norway's Nokia and Sweden's Ericsson are taking 5G business away from Huawei.

Yet, in order to do so, Japanese companies themselves need to regain their strength. To do this, it is important to remove the impediments of the past 30 years. In my view, the biggest impediment is the consumption tax.

So let us try to gain some insight by comparing Japan's tax revenue structure with that of Denmark and Sweden, which have the highest consumption tax rates in the world.

35. Tax revenue trend of Japan

Chart 34: Japan's Tax Revenue Trends and Tax Revenue of Other Countries (Source: OECD)

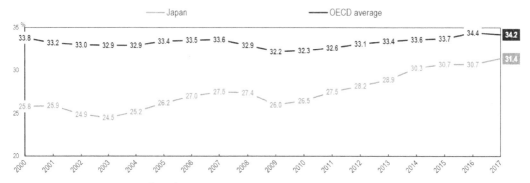

Tax-to-GDP ratio compared to the OECD, 2017

The chart below shows tax-to-GDP ratios for 2018. As Japan is unable to provide 2018 data, the latest available data from 2017 has been used. Japan's 2017 tax-to-GDP ratio ranked it 25th out of 36 OECD countries in terms of the tax-to-GDP ratio compared with the 2018 figures. In 2017 Japan had a tax-to-GDP ratio of 31.4%, compared with the OECD average of 34.3% in 2018 and 34.2% in 2017. In 2017 Japan was ranked 26th out of 36 OECD countries in terms of the tax-to-GDP ratio.

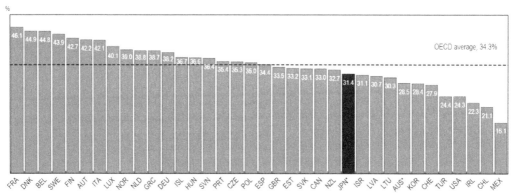

* Australia and Japan are unable to provide provisional 2018 data, therefore their latest 2017 data are presented within this country note.

The line chart in the upper part of Chart 34 shows the ratio of tax revenue to GDP for OECD countries from 2000 to 2017. The dark line is the average of the 36 OECD countries, and the light line is for Japan. Japan's tax revenue as a percentage of GDP has been consistently low, but as of 2017, it has risen to 31.4%. However, the average for the 36 OECD countries is 34.2%, which means it is still relatively low.

The bottom bars show a country-by-country comparison of tax revenues as a percentage of GDP in 2018 for 36 OECD countries. Only Japan and Australia have figures for 2017, and Japan is indicated as a dark bar. This shows that Japan is ranked 25th. On the other hand, the average for the 36 OECD countries has risen from 34.2% in 2017 to 34.3%.

36. Tax revenue structure of Japan

Chart 35: Tax revenue structure of Japan (Source: OECD)

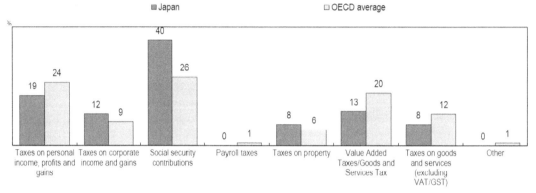

Chart 35 compares Japan's tax revenue sources in 2017 with the OECD average for similar tax revenue sources. The dark bars of each pair are those of Japan. The light bars are those of the OECD average. Japan does not have payroll tax and others.

It is important to note that Japan's largest source of tax revenue is social security contributions, which account for 40% of tax receipts in the broad sense. Social security is a generic term for medical insurance, pension insurance, nursing care insurance, worker's compensation insurance, and unemployment insurance. In other words, Japan's consumption tax, which is supposed to be a source of funding for social security, is positioned as a supplementary source of revenue. Therefore, it has become necessary to look at the balance of payments for social security expenses, which is separate from the general account finances seen in Chart 01 above. This will be discussed in the next chapter, "The Social Security System on the Eve of Collapse."

What we can learn from Chart 35 is that when 40% of social insurance premium revenue, 21% of the consumption tax revenue, and 8% of property tax revenue are combined, nearly 70% of Japan's tax revenue is collected in a manner similar to a stable source of revenue with little fluctuation due to the economy. However, as mentioned earlier, stable revenue sources carry a greater risk of prolonging the recession by collecting taxes without mercy even when the economy is bad. On the contrary, even when the economy is good, there is no significant upside.

In addition, when it comes to social security contributions, Japan collects more than 1.5 times as much as the OECD average. This suggests that even if we try to cut spending to restore government finances, it will be difficult without addressing the social security system.

However, as we will see later, the social security system is already on the verge of collapse, and spending cuts are unthinkable. This means that instead of trying to reduce social insurance premium income, it is inevitable to increase tax revenue from income tax and corporate tax that have less risk of recession out of those taxes mentioned above. The reason why these two have less risk of recession is that they levy on salaries and profits resulting from business operations on a results basis.

Then, what about Denmark, which has the highest consumption tax rate (value-added tax rate) along with Sweden, as seen in Chart 33 above?

37. Tax revenue trend of Denmark

Chart 36: Denmark's Tax Revenue Trends and Tax Revenue of Other Countries (Source: OECD)

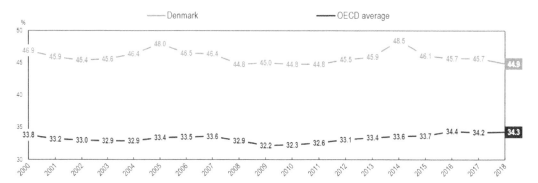

Tax-to-GDP ratio compared to the OECD, 2018

Denmark ranked 2nd out of 36 OECD countries in terms of the tax-to-GDP ratio in 2018. In 2018, Denmark had a tax-to-GDP ratio of 44.9% compared with the OECD average of 34.3%. In 2017, Denmark was also ranked 2nd out of the 36 OECD countries in terms of the tax-to-GDP ratio.

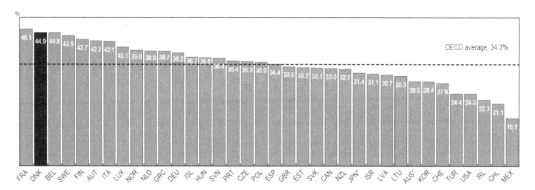

* Australia and Japan are unable to provide provisional 2018 data, therefore their latest 2017 data are presented within this country note

The line chart in the upper part of Chart 36 shows the tax revenues of OECD countries as a percentage of GDP from 2000 to 2018. The dark line is the average of the 36 OECD countries and the light line is for Denmark. It can be seen that Denmark's tax revenue as a percentage of GDP has been consistently high.

The bottom bars show a country-by-country comparison of tax revenues as a percentage of GDP for 36 OECD countries in 2018. Denmark is indicated as a dark bar. This shows that Denmark, the country with the highest consumption tax rate along with Sweden, had a tax revenue of 44.9% of GDP in 2018, ranking second only to France.

According to the basic data of the Kingdom of Denmark on the website of the Ministry of Foreign Affairs, the country's economy is as follows.

(Start of quote)

1, Main industries
Wholesale and retail, pharmaceuticals, livestock and agriculture, transportation, energy

2, GDP
350.9 billion dollars (IMF statistics, 2018)

3, GDP per capita
60,692 USD (IMF statistics, 2018)

4, Economic growth rate
1.2% (IMF statistics, 2018)

5, Price inflation rate
0.7% (IMF statistics, 2018)

6, Unemployment rate
5.0% (IMF statistics, 2018)

7, Total trade value
(1) Exports: $107.9 billion
(2) Imports: $101.4 billion
(Statistics Denmark, 2018)

8, Main trade goods

(1) Exports: Pharmaceuticals, industrial machinery and its parts, apparel

(2) Imports: Automobiles, petroleum and petroleum products, electrical equipment and parts thereof

(Statistics Denmark, 2018)

9, Major trading partners

(1) Exports: Germany (15.9%), Sweden (9.9%), United States (8.6%), China (4.4%), Japan (1.4%)

(2) Imports: Germany (23.0%), Sweden (12.3%), Netherlands (8.5%), China (7.7%) ···· Japan (0.5%)

(Statistics Denmark, 2018)

10, Currency

Danish krone

Economic Overview

(1) Recent Economic Conditions

In Denmark, the GDP growth rate fell to -5.7% in 2009 due to the global financial crisis and a decline in exports caused by falling external demand. However, the economy showed a recovery trend thanks to strong exports and domestic demand, and the growth rate in 2017 was 2.1%, the highest in the past 10 years. In 2018, the growth rate dropped to 1.2% due to a decrease in agricultural production caused by the heat wave, but it is expected to pick up to around 2% in 2019 and beyond.

(2) Labor Force Shortage

In 2008, the country recorded a historically low unemployment rate of 3.5%, but the rate later rose to the mid-7% range after 2010 due to the global financial crisis. Since then, the government has promoted export promotion and vocational training policies, and the employment situation has improved; however, the unemployment rate for 2018 is 5.0% (IMF statistics), and labor shortages are becoming more apparent in some industries such as construction.

(3) Fiscal situation

The government's public finances, which had been in surplus and sound since 2004, reflecting the strong economy, fell into deficit in the fourth quarter of 2008, triggered by the global financial crisis, but has since recovered, with outstanding government debt (national and local) at 34.3% of GDP in 2018 (IMF statistics).

(4) Euro participation issue

In a referendum held in September 2000, 53.1% of the votes were against and 46.9% were in favor of joining the euro, and Denmark is not currently a member of the euro. However, as a participant in the European Exchange Rate Mechanism (ERM II), Denmark has adopted a policy of keeping the fluctuation range of its currency against the euro within 2.25% above or below the central exchange rate, effectively adopting a fixed exchange rate system with the euro.

(Note: translated by Arata Yaguchi)

(End of quote)

While Denmark has the highest consumption tax rate in the world, it has a GDP per capita of $60,692 (IMF statistics, 2018), which is 1.55 times higher than Japan's $39,082 (IMF, 2018). In addition, Denmark's economic growth rate for 2019 according to the IMF is 2.35% growth, which is much higher than Japan's 0.67% growth.

38. Tax revenue structure of Denmark

Chart 37: Tax revenue structure of Denmark (Source: OECD)

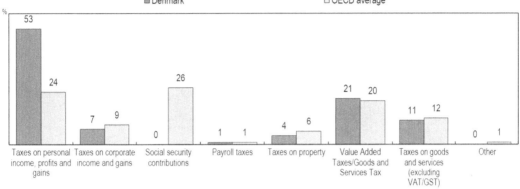

In the tax revenue structure seen in Chart 37, the dark bars of each pair are those of Denmark. The light bars are those of the OECD average.

The weight of the consumption tax revenue is on par with the OECD average, but income tax revenue is large. And the social security contribution is zero. Now, about the Danish social security system, which does not collect social insurance premiums, I quote directly from the Danish Embassy page on Facebook, as of April 2, 2017.

(Start of quote)

[The relationship between Denmark's generous social security system and its financial resources and burdens]

Denmark's generous social security system, which includes the following, is one of the reasons why Danes feel they are among the happiest countries in the world.

1. Medical care is free of charge, as well as home nursing care and overseas medical care when necessary. Family members who need to accompany and care for the patient will also receive income protection.

2. Nursing care and other necessary services are provided free of charge, 24 hours a day, at home. Wheelchairs and other necessary equipment will be provided free of charge.

3. All citizens are entitled to a basic pension of about 200,000 yen per month.

4. Child allowance is from 14,000 yen to 22,000 yen per month. Maternity and childcare leave is available for a total of approximately one year.

5. Education is free up to graduate school. All students receive a monthly benefit close to 100,000 yen (if living separately from parents).

On the other hand, these generous programs are covered by a heavier tax burden than in Japan.

Income tax is 35-48% on average (less than 10% in Japan), consumption tax is 25% (8% in Japan), and there are no reduced tax rates, including for food. On the other hand, corporate taxes are kept low at 22% in Denmark, compared to about 30% in Japan. The tax system is designed to be neutral to economic activities, with more freedom in the upstream of wealth-generating economic activities.

Furthermore, social security is entirely funded by taxes, and not by an insurance system like in Japan (there is no premium burden for health and nursing care insurance or pension insurance). Therefore, unlike, for example, the national pension insurance premiums, where a fixed amount of money is paid regardless of income, in Denmark all citizens pay their fair share, while social security benefits are equalized so that those who need them can receive the necessary services for free, regardless of wealth. There is no such thing as a "no pension" because you did not have insurance.

A high income tax rate and a consumption tax with no reduction rate may seem regressive (heavy burden on low income earners), but in Japan, part-time and non-

regular workers may not be able to get social insurance, whereas in Denmark, since taxes are the source of funds, all necessary people can receive necessary social security services, and as a result the income redistribution function of social security is the best functioning in the world (the gap between the rich and the poor is small).

In addition, since the same consumption tax rate is applied regardless of the item, the problem of political intervention regarding the items to which the reduced tax rate is applied and the complexity of tax collection calculations are avoided.

To sum up the above, although the burden is high, with a relatively simple burden, everyone can receive the necessary social security equally. For this reason, high welfare and high burden are accepted by the people in Denmark, I guess.

The Danish people may have a strong sense of attachment and patriotism toward their country due to both a sense of security in their lives through such social security and a sense that they are contributing to society by paying taxes.

(Note: translated by Arata Yaguchi)

(End of quote)

The point is "the equal system in which all citizens pay their fair share, while social security benefits are provided free of charge to those who need them regardless of wealth," isn't it?

In addition, although the tax burden is considered to be higher as the income tax rate and the consumption tax rate are higher than in Japan, the total of stable source of revenue, such as property tax revenue, consumption value-added tax revenue and consumption tax (excluding value-added tax) revenue, is only 36%, as 4%, 21% and 11% respectively, which is almost half lower than in Japan.

The fact that Denmark's tax system is a retributive rather than a flat-rate system, and that it has the smallest gap between rich and poor in the world, seems to contribute to its economic stability and the happiness of its citizens.

Next, let's take a look at Sweden, which along with Denmark has the highest consumption tax rate (value-added tax rate).

39. Tax revenue trend of Sweden

Chart 38: Sweden's Tax Revenue Trends and Tax Revenue of Other Countries (Source: OECD)

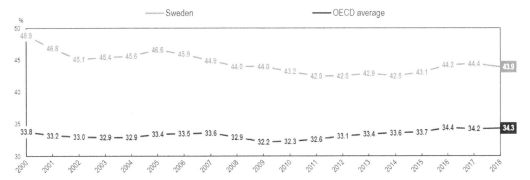

Tax-to-GDP ratio compared to the OECD, 2018

Sweden ranked 4th out of 36 OECD countries in terms of the tax-to-GDP ratio in 2018. In 2018, Sweden had a tax-to-GDP ratio of 43.9% compared with the OECD average of 34.3%. In 2017, Sweden was also ranked 4th out of the 36 OECD countries in terms of the tax-to-GDP ratio.

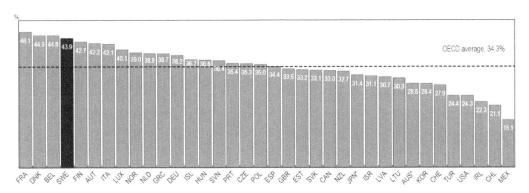

* Australia and Japan are unable to provide provisional 2018 data, therefore their latest 2017 data are presented within this country note

The line chart in the upper part of Chart 38 shows tax revenues as a percentage of GDP for OECD countries from 2000 to 2018. The dark line is the average of the 36 OECD countries and the light line is for Sweden. It can be seen that Sweden, the country with the highest consumption tax rate along with Denmark, has consistently high tax revenue as a percentage of GDP.

The bottom bars show a country-by-country comparison of tax revenues as a percentage of GDP for 36 OECD countries in 2018. Sweden is indicated as a dark bar. This shows that Sweden's tax revenue in 2018 was 43.9% of GDP, ranking the fourth among OECD countries.

The economy of Sweden according to the basic data of the Kingdom of Sweden on the website of the Ministry of Foreign Affairs is as follows.

(Start quote)

1. Main Industries
Machinery industry (including automobiles), chemical industry, forestry, IT

2. GDP
551.1 billion dollars (IMF, 2018)

3. GDP per capita
53,873 USD (2018, IMF)

4. Economic growth rate
2.3% (2018, IMF)

5. Price inflation rate
2.0% (IMF, 2018)

6. Unemployment rate
6.2% (IMF, 2018)

7. Total trade value
(1) Exports 135,523 million euro
(2) Imports: 136,301 million euros
*   (2017, Eurostat)*

8. Major trade items
(1) Exports: Machinery, transportation equipment other than railroad, electrical

equipment, mineral fuels, paper and pulp.
(2) Import: Machinery, electrical equipment, transportation equipment other than railroad, mineral fuels, plastics

9. Major trading partners
(1) Exports: Germany, Norway, Finland, Denmark, U.S.A.
(2) Imports: Germany, Netherlands, Norway, Denmark, United Kingdom
   (Statistics Sweden, 2018)

10. Currency
Swedish krona (SEK)

Economic Overview

(1) Economic situation
The economic growth rate was sluggish in 2012 and 2013 due to the turmoil in the global economy caused by the European debt crisis and other factors, but recorded high growth from 2014 onward, with the economic growth rate of 4.5% in 2015, 2.7% in 2016, and 2.1% in 2017. We expect moderate economic growth to continue in 2018 and beyond. (Figures from IMF).

(2) Employment situation
The unemployment rate is improving, with 299,000 unemployed in November 2018 and an unemployment rate of 5.5% (figures from Statistics Sweden); employment growth is expected to slow from 2019 onwards.

(3) Fiscal and monetary policy
In December 2018, the 2019 government budget, presented to parliament by the center-right opposition Moderate and Christian Democrat parties, was adopted. It emphasizes employment and growth policies with an emphasis on liberal reforms, strengthening law and order, integrating immigrants by improving education, etc., improving the health care system, enhancing the education system, and addressing the elderly by reducing taxes for pensioners.

After reaching 0% for the first time in history in October 2014, the central bank decided to introduce negative interest rates and purchase government bonds in stages in February 2015. The repo rate was kept at minus 0.50% until December 2018, when it was raised to minus 0.25% in January 2019.

(4) Government Economic Outlook
*   2018 2019 2020*
* GDP growth rate (real) 2.2% 1.3% 1.7%*
* Unemployment rate (age 16-74) 6.3% 6.4% 6.5%*
* Consumer price inflation (CPI) 1.9% 2.0% 2.1%*
* (Source: Swedish Agency for Economic Analysis, December 2018)*

(Note: translated by Arata Yaguchi)

(End quote)

This shows that while Sweden has the highest consumption tax rate in the world, its GDP per capita is $53,873 (IMF, 2018), which is 1.38 times higher than Japan's $39,082 (IMF, 2018). In addition, Sweden's economic growth rate for 2019 according to the IMF is 1.26% growth, which is higher than Japan's 0.67% growth.

40. Tax revenue structure of Sweden

Chart 39: Tax revenue structure of Sweden (Source: OECD)

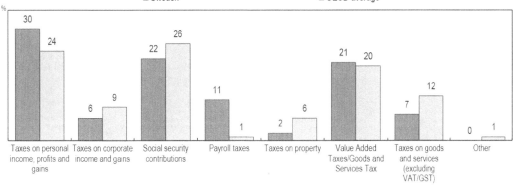

In the tax revenue structure in Chart 39, the dark bars are those of Sweden. The light bars are those of the OECD average.

The consumption tax revenue, together with VAT, accounts for 28% of total tax revenue; the OECD average is 32%, indicating a low dependence on the consumption tax despite the highest rate. The highest percentage of tax revenue is income tax revenue of 30%, and when combined with 11% of payroll tax revenue, the figure is 41%. While the total stable source of revenue, which combined with 28% of consumption tax revenue, 2% of property tax revenue, and 22% of social insurance premium revenue, is 52%, lower than Japan but higher than Denmark.

Comparing the tax revenues of these three countries, Denmark relies most on the productive power of its citizens, followed by Sweden. Japan, on the other hand, does not rely on the productive power of its citizens, but relies most on a stable source of revenue that it collects even during economic downturns. The fact that the power of economic growth is in this order may suggest that Japan may be able to regain its growth potential by changing its tax system to one that believes in the productive power of the people.

Denmark and Sweden, which are said to have the highest tax burdens, are, on the other hand, regular members of the world's most livable countries. The fact that the social security system in Japan, which has the highest social security burden, is wobbly, while the social security systems in Denmark and Sweden, which have the highest income tax revenues, are robust, suggests that if we improve the safety net and create an environment in which the people can take risks, both the people and the government are likely to gain returns as the economy grows faster, incomes grow and income taxes increase.

41. Government spending in 32 OECD countries

Chart 40: Comparison of OECD governments' total expenditures (Source: Ministry of Finance)

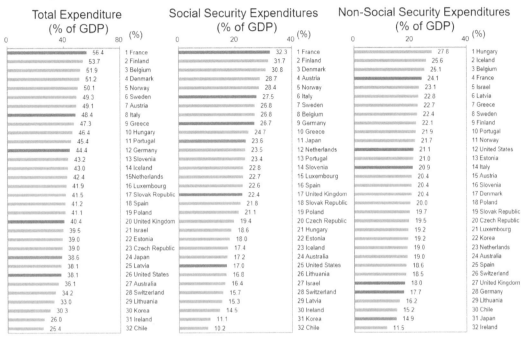

Chart 40 shows a comparison of the expenditure side of the governments of the 32 OECD countries. The dark bars are those of G5 countries including Japan. The total expenditure of the Japanese government is 38.6% of GDP, which is below the middle rank. In addition, the Japanese government's social security expenditure is 23.6% of GDP, which is only slightly higher than the OECD average, even though it collects more than 60% of its total tax revenue in the broad sense of the word in the form of social insurance premiums. Still, the government is not cutting back on social security spending, with other expenditures at 14.9%, second from the bottom. This implies that Japan does not have enough tax revenue.

The Japanese government, with its below-average tax revenue, naturally cannot spend much. Even so, it is difficult to cut back on social security spending, so the government is cutting back on other spending, such as education. This is one of the reasons why Japan's competitiveness has been declining.

In terms of total expenditure, Denmark ranks fourth and Sweden the sixth. Social security expenditures are also high, with Denmark in third place and Sweden in seventh. In other words, they earn relatively large amounts and spend large amounts to create a prosperous and comfortable country to live in. On the other hand, as Japan's tax revenue peaked in fiscal 1990, it can be said that the country's tax system has destined it to be poor.

I see the possibility that the dependence on income tax, which takes from where it can and when it can, is linked to the stability of the social security system, which gives to where it cannot, and to the well-being of the people.

42. Trends in the fiscal balance of Japan, Denmark and Sweden

Chart 41: Trends in the fiscal balance of Japan, Denmark and Sweden (Source: OECD)

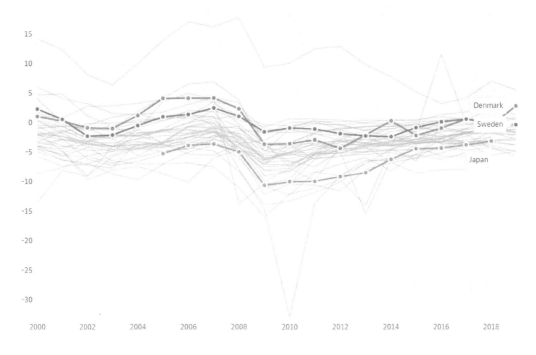

Chart 41 shows the fiscal balance as a percentage of GDP for Japan, Denmark, and Sweden since 2000.

While Japan has been in negative territory for a long time, the two countries have been hovering around zero, which indicates equilibrium. If the surplus increases, it can be returned to the people by increasing spending, as seen in the previous Chart 40, so keeping the surplus within plus or minus 5% of GDP, as in the two countries, may be said to be ideal fiscal management. In other words, the governments of both countries have continued to manage their economies well.

The excellence of the two countries' economic management is also reflected in their outstanding government debt, which is indicated by the arrows in Chart 42 below. Both are at a level slightly above 50% of GDP. Incidentally, that of Japan is on the far right.

Due to the high consumption tax rate, readers may have had the impression that the social security systems in Denmark and Sweden are enhanced in exchange for a heavy tax burden. Wouldn't you have thought of them as lackluster societies with more equality than competition? Or have you heard from people who live in both countries, or traveled there yourself, that it is gloomy and dark? However, I put more value on the numbers than on such impressions.

For example, have you ever encountered professional fund managers and analysts talking about what they have seen in the real place, and emphasizing their professional superiority by saying don't talk about things without seeing the real place, and don't invest without talking to the president?

But how much do you know about the town you live in or the company you work for, if that is what you are led to believe? At the time of Japan's financial crisis in 1997, there was even a person who had become the CEO of a failed company who did not know the actual condition of the company until he took office. He hadn't even look at the numbers.

I lived in Melbourne, New York and London for a combined total of about 10 years. but the figures available on the Internet give me much more information about the places. The U.S. figures are particularly rich, and I can say that I know more about the U.S. economy as a whole than most Americans who actually live there.

People and impressions lie. Numbers also lie, but it is easier to find inconsistencies in numerical lies. At least they are much easier to spot than people and impressions. What I am trying to say here is that anyone can be armed with data. Anyone can debunk the lie that the consumption tax is necessary to maintain the social security system.

I've never been to Denmark or Sweden. To tell the truth, I've always had a gloomy image of the country and had no desire to visit. However, the figures presented here give me the impression of a society where there is no need to fear failure, rather than the image of a heavy tax burden and equality rather than competition. I think that's why the people have been able to achieve positive results there. The numbers tell me that both countries seem to be quite good countries.

Chart 42: Outstanding government debt in Japan, Denmark and Sweden (Source: OECD data with arrows inserted)

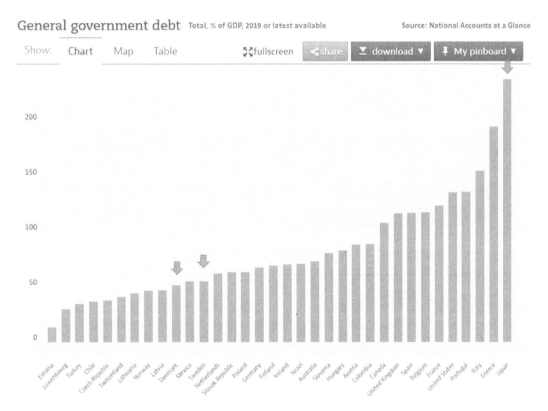

43. Trends in income tax rates in major economies

Chart 43: Trends in income tax rates in major countries (Source: Ministry of Finance)

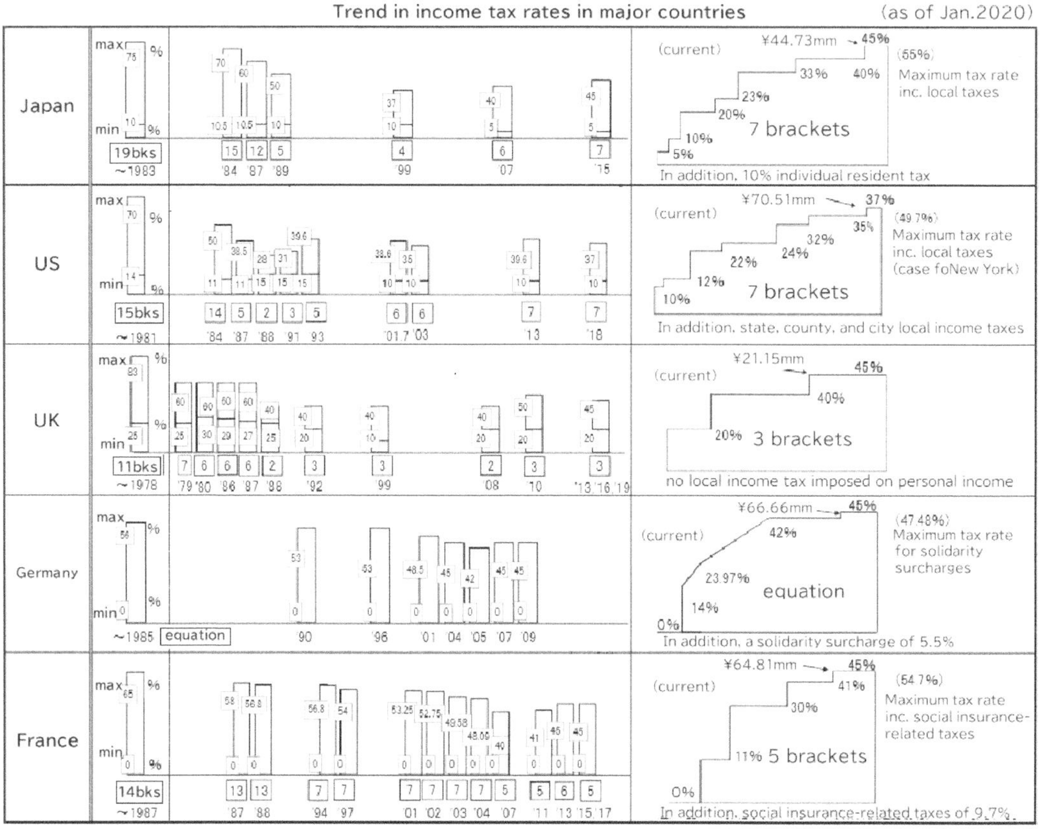

(Note: translated by Arata Yaguchi)

Chart 43 shows the income tax rates of the G5 countries from around 1980 to the present. From top to bottom, Japan, the United States, the United Kingdom, Germany, and France.

While the trends in consumption tax rates around the world seen in the previous Chart 33 generally rose steadily, the trends in income tax rates in major countries seen on the left side of Chart 43 have generally fallen steadily. This suggests that these major countries have tried to secure financial resources to cut taxes on high-income earners by raising consumption tax rates, which are considered harsh on low-income earners. In other words, each country has adopted a tax system that leads to the widening of the gap between the rich and the poor.

This is possible because money can drive politics. It is possible because money can be used to manipulate information. It is possible to create a certain impression with money.

Having seen this data, I am now keenly aware that the tax system is the foundation of a country's economy. Looking back on the history of Japan, we can see that things such as the annual tribute and "rakuichi rakuza" can be described as special zones for tax systems and tax incentives, and they have had a great deal to do with the rise and fall of local economies.

The widening gap between the rich and the poor has had a negative impact on the economy, as it has reduced the purchasing power of the majority while allowing the few to accumulate unusable wealth. The extreme widening of the gap between the rich and the poor gives the few the comparable power of a nation, while creating more desperate people and destabilizing society. There is an urgent need to examine the existing tax system and reverse it to one that promotes income transfer from the wealthy to the general public.

44. Global trends in corporate tax rates

Chart 44: Average statutory corporate tax rates by geographic region around the world (Source: OECD)

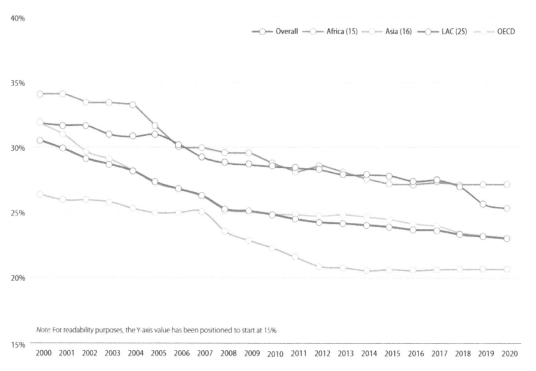

Chart 44 shows the statutory average corporate tax rate by region in the world from 2000 to 2020. The top line shows the average corporate tax rate for African countries, the second for Latin America, the third for OECD, the forth for the world as a whole, and the bottom line for Asian countries. Incidentally, of the 36 OECD countries, Hungary now has the lowest corporate tax rate at 9%, followed by Ireland at 12.5%.

This shows that the decline in corporate tax rates has been a global phenomenon. Have companies in these countries used the money generated by the tax cuts to raise labor costs, invest in equipment, and spend on research and development, thereby increasing their competitiveness? Or have the managers monopolized most of the available funds? I would like to think that OECD countries, including Japan, have generally been in the former category.

What is ironic, however, is that despite the fact that the reduction in Japan's corporate tax rate has been one of the most rapid, it has not led to an increase in the competitiveness of Japanese companies, but rather has resulted in a loss of competitiveness, as shown in Chart 23 above. However, the lowering of the corporate tax rate cannot be the cause of the decline in competitiveness; there must have been other major causes. You the readers who have read this far can see that the consumption tax may have reduced the competitiveness of companies through the economic recession.

However, as we have learned through Denmark and Sweden, it is not necessarily only high consumption tax rates that inhibit economic growth. It can be said that the "weight of the household's fixed burden," which is a balance between income and other taxes such as social insurance premiums, inhibits economic growth.

45. Only a handful of countries have budget surpluses

Chart 45: Trends in fiscal balance of OECD countries (Source: OECD)

Chart 45 shows the fiscal balance as a percentage of GDP in OECD countries since 1995. In addition to Japan, the other two countries highlighted are Norway, with a large upturn, and Ireland, with a large downturn. It can be seen that Norway has enjoyed budget surpluses on the back of oil revenues. On the other hand, Ireland's budget deficit skyrocketed due to its "rule-breaking" fiscal stimulus in the Eurozone in response to the rapid deterioration of the housing market in the aftermath of the U.S. subprime mortgage crisis and the post-Lehman shock recession.

The subprime shock was the bursting of the housing bubble in the U.S. It occurred in the summer of 2007 and the market rapidly deteriorated, so in September of the same year the U.S. Federal Reserve Bank (FRB) lowered its policy interest rate from 5.25% to 4.75%, and subsequently lowered it by 5.25%

in a little over a year, to 0% in December 2008. In Europe, this was mainly spread to the UK, Ireland, and Spain. In response, the Bank of England (BOE) lowered the rate from 5.75% to 5.50% in December 2007, and also made a 5.25% reduction in a little over a year, to 0.5% in March 2009. However, the European Central Bank (ECB) of the Eurozone, a joint family of countries, raised its interest rate from 4.0% to 4.25% in July 2008. And the rate cut would have to wait until after the Lehman shock in October of the same year, when it was lowered from 4.25% to 3.75%.

At the time of the subprime mortgage crisis, the largest financial institution in the world was Lehman Brothers. Lehman Brothers had made significant profits for at least the previous several years by selling mortgage backed securities based on subprime loans. So when many investors and its industry peers began to sell such bonds, Lehman Brothers was the one to buy them in order to support the market.

When a bubble bursts, it is often the biggest players in the industry that suffer the most, largely because they own the most and cannot sell, and have the ability to support the market for some time.

Chart 46 below shows the policy rates of Japan, the United States, Eurozone, and the United Kingdom from January 2007 to May 2009. The rapid interest rate cuts by the FRB seen after the subprime mortgage crisis indicate that the U.S. perception of the crisis was far from normal.

The U.K. also shares the sense of crisis, but we can see that it was only after the collapse of Lehman Brothers that it realized the seriousness of the situation. In the case of the Bank of Japan, it can be seen that there was already little room for interest rate cuts. This is because, as mentioned above, the rate has remained below 0.50% since March 1997.

What can also be seen here is that even though the US and UK central banks cut interest rates during the recession after the subprime shock, the ECB did the opposite and raised rates, mainly because of the high rate of inflation in Germany. As a result, the economic downturn in Ireland and Spain, which were the most affected by the subprime shock in the Eurozone, accelerated.

Chart 46: Trends in policy rates in Japan, the U.S., Europe, and the U.K. (Source: Compiled from these Central Banks data)

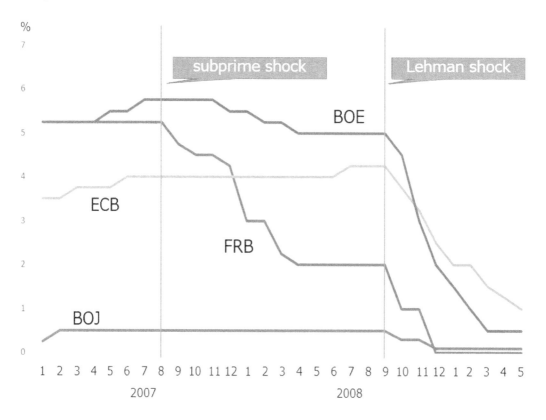

The Eurozone has a rule that mandates that each country's budget deficit must be kept within 3% of GDP. However, in 2008, five countries - France, Spain, Greece, Ireland, and Malta - broke the 3% limit in response to the economic downturn. As a result, these five countries were forced to implement austerity measures despite the economic crisis. However, Ireland was the only country that dared to "break the rule" and rush to stimulate the economy. This is the reason for the sharp increase in the deficit seen in Chart 45.

Chart 47 below shows the real GDP growth rates of the major Eurozone countries from 2007 to 2015. The line chart with the steepest upward angle is that of Ireland. The most depressed one is that of Greece. The rest of the countries have basically not deviated significantly. This is not a coincidence, as the countries of the Eurozone have been working to integrate their currencies and monetary policies so that their macroeconomic figures do not diverge significantly. The rule requiring that budget deficits be limited to 3% of GDP was also said to be a stepping stone toward future fiscal integration.

Chart 47: Trends in real GDP growth rates of major Eurozone countries (Source: OECD data)

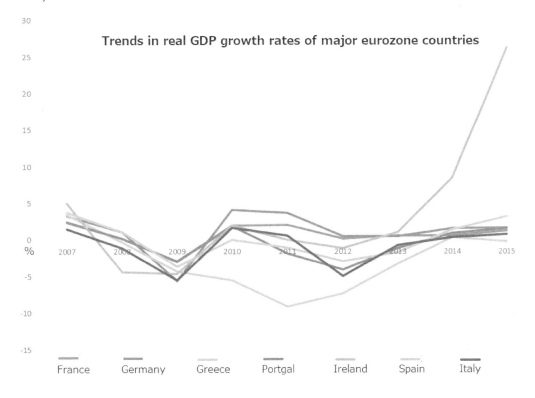

What Chart 47 suggests is that breaking the rules in an emergency is also a necessary evil for survival. Rules are usually made in peacetime and are not predicated on ruin. This implies that a decision to break the rules may be required when it is determined that following the rules will lead to ruin. As a result of such rule-breaking risk-taking, Ireland has seen returns in the form of a rapid economic recovery. It also achieved fiscal balance by 2019, as seen in Chart 45 above.

Please take a closer look at Chart 46 again. In the aftermath of the subprime mortgage crisis, the United Kingdom and Ireland, two neighboring countries, both suffered. Therefore, the U.K. followed the U.S. in lowering its interest rate, while Ireland as a member of the Eurozone raised its interest rate for the convenience of the organization. It could be argued that for the Irish government to even follow the fiscal rules of the Eurozone here would be an act of betrayal of the people. Nevertheless, while most continental countries followed the organization's lead, the Irish government protected its people. Isn't it possible that these circumstances led to the later Brexit in the neighboring country? The UK is not a member of the Eurozone, so it can make its own monetary policy, but as a member of the EU at the time, many of its policies were tailored to the needs of the organization.

Nevertheless, corporations, which have been given preferential treatment by lowering the corporate tax rate, have worked to widen the income gap in real terms by increasing the number of non-regular workers while increasing the compensation of managers within those companies. And although governments have raised the consumption tax rates to make up for the decline in corporate tax revenues, as seen in Chart 45, only a handful of countries have budget surpluses, and many have budget deficits. And we know that the fiscal situation of all countries have deteriorated further in 2020, while the wealth gap widened.

This suggests that the tax system during this period was a system of wealth accumulation for the wealthy via income transfer from individuals to the government. It is no coincidence that a few billionaires have come to monopolize the world's wealth. On the other hand, the government's finances are supported by the people as a whole, but since the OECD average for corporate tax revenue is 9%, this means that more than 90% is supported by individuals. Under the current tax system, 90% of the growing budget deficits of each country will continue to be borne by the general public.

One of the main themes at the World Economic Forum over the past several years has always been the issue of wealth inequality. I don't know what has been discussed there. However, as we have seen, there is a very high possibility that the world's tax system has increased the gap between the rich and the poor. This is because they have reduced taxes on corporations and high-income earners while ensuring that they are collected from low-income earners, such as consumption taxes and social insurance premiums.

In particular, Japan's consumption tax worsens the economy, reduces total tax revenue, and increases inequality. Increasing inequality leads to increasing social security costs. Isn't this what we're stuck with?

46. Value of currency

Chart 48: Factors that determine the value of a currency

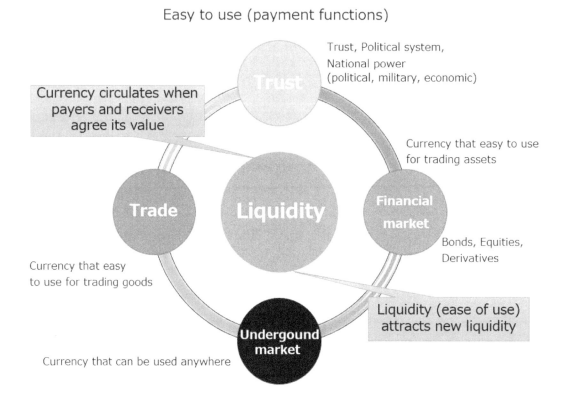

Chart 48 was created by myself, who worked as a foreign exchange dealer for many years, to explain what the value of currency is for investors and others. In order to understand the inflation rate and fiscal balance discussed in this book, I feel the need to explain what currency is.

The essential value of a currency, as I see it, is liquidity. High liquidity means the ability to buy and sell at any time, in any place, in any quantity, on a more stable basis; another way of describing it is "easy-to-use". The four elements that support liquidity are the trust provided by the issuing country, the settlement function in trade, the openness and size of the financial market, and the convenience of being received by anyone, including the black market. Also, even if the payer wants to use a certain currency, he cannot do so if the recipient refuses to accept it. Or, even if the recipient does accept the currency, for instance, the payment in Japanese yen may be more expensive than the payment in U.S. dollars, as you may experience when traveling abroad. It is necessary for both parties to accept the value of the currency.

And once high liquidity is established, it will always attract new liquidity because of its convenience. In this sense, if I should specify the most established currency, the position of the U.S. dollar is unlikely to be challenged by any other currency.

Cryptocurrencies at the moment also have a lack of liquidity. Apart from being circulated within exchanges, even if providers of goods and services accept payments in cryptocurrencies at the moment, there is no guarantee that this will continue for any length of time. If no one accepts them in commercial transactions, they run the risk of suddenly becoming worthless outside the exchange. This is because shops or makers can't accept more than a certain amount of payments because if they accept something as volatile as cryptocurrency, their sales and profits will swing wildly.

In addition, with more than 400 exchanges and more than 6,000 types of cryptocurrencies, there is limited potential for liquidity to increase on an unconsolidated basis. In this sense, it must be said that the usability of cryptocurrencies is extremely poor, except for those who are directly involved in mining and trading.

So how about legal tender?

I have traveled to Russia, Ukraine and Poland during the former Soviet Union era, where the US dollar was in circulation in the black market, because even the locals could buy many things there with US dollars that they could not with the local currency. The ruble and zloty at that time were less liquid than the US dollar, both inside and outside the country. The main reason for this lack of liquidity may be "trust" that the system was inhibiting free trade and the economic power was greatly substandard.

The essential value of currency is liquidity. Liquidity is enhanced if it is easy to use and if the payer and receiver can easily agree on the value. A major scoring point for this is that it must be issued by a reliable state and be stable for use in trade and financial markets. Such high liquidity is also easy to use in the black market, which again increases liquidity.

So what is a low value currency from this perspective?

The first is a currency with a high inflation rate. Since the inflation rate is also an indicator of the purchasing power of a currency, a high inflation rate directly indicates a depreciation of the currency.

The second is the currency that you are forced to convert to another country's currency when you use it. While some currencies, such as the dollar, can be used in many countries, there are many currencies that can hardly be used outside of one's own country. Also, in trade and investment, if the size of the home country is small, it is forced to convert to other currencies. This means that the currency is exposed to greater exchange rate risk.

And it is a currency whose exchange rate is expected to be unfavourable due to creditworthiness and other factors. It can be used and held with confidence in trade and capital transactions if the government guarantees free trade and it has the ability to maintain the guarantee.

In this way, we can see that huge accumulated deficits and public debt, as well as a money supply that exceeds that of the real economy, are factors that cause currencies to lose value through the deterioration of creditworthiness and inherent concerns about inflation.

There is a theory, like MMT (Modern Monetary Theory), that depending on the situation, there is no need to worry about budget deficits. If this were true, then the tax revenue needed to reduce budget deficits would not be needed. Countries around the world would stop collecting taxes, stop recording and reporting their confusing fiscal accounts, and simply print their money. This is an excellent idea for countries with large accumulated deficits and public debts, including the Japanese government, but is it really the right way to go?

The main points of MMT, as far as I know, are as follows.

1. The government can print and spend as much currency as it wants as long as there is no inflation.
2. Don't worry about budget deficits, because the currency issued by the government does not decrease with use like personal assets.
3. When inflation occurs, it suggests that the government is issuing too much currency, at which time taxes are raised to absorb the money.
4. The reason why the government needs tax is to prevent the risk of inflation.
5. However, MMT only applies to governments that control their own currency, and does not work for countries that borrow in another currency. In other words, it cannot be applied to Eurozone countries because they do not have their own currency, and it cannot be applied to countries with foreign currency debt, such as Argentina and Lebanon, which defaulted in 2020.

Nevertheless, legal tender circulates as currency because the issuing country has creditworthiness. This creditworthiness is the basis for liquidity and supports the value of the currency. How long will other countries tolerate a country printing as much currency as it needs to pay its trade and debt obligations?

In this way, the currency issued by the government will also depreciate, just like personal assets. If it comes out of thin air, like a magic trick, then depreciation of the currency is inevitable. More currency means less credit. This depreciation will eventually be realized through higher import prices. In fact, the main point of MMT, "1. The government can print and spend as much currency as it needs as long as it does not cause inflation." suggests that MMT will end up inducing inflation. Thus, when inflation arrives due to a decline in external credit, raising taxes only domestically will not only be completely ineffective, but will also lead to the destruction of the people's livelihood.

As discussed in Section 32, "How about in terms of net debt outstanding?", the reason why the Japanese government has been able to maintain its credibility even with the world's worst huge accumulated deficit and public debt is because of the private assets having been accumulated by Japanese people.

MMT could work until it erodes its creditworthiness, which would mean that the government would entirely exhaust the assets of the people.

As we saw in the previous section, even by 2019 there were few countries in the world with budget surpluses, but this situation was certain to worsen in 2020. If MMT is anything like that of my understanding, then it seems to me that the background to the increased attention reflects the "A drowning man will clutch at a straw." sentiment of governments.

Chapter 3: The Social Security System on the Eve of Collapse

47. Japan's public social security expenditures

Chart 49: Public social security expenditure in OECD countries (Source: OECD data with arrows inserted)

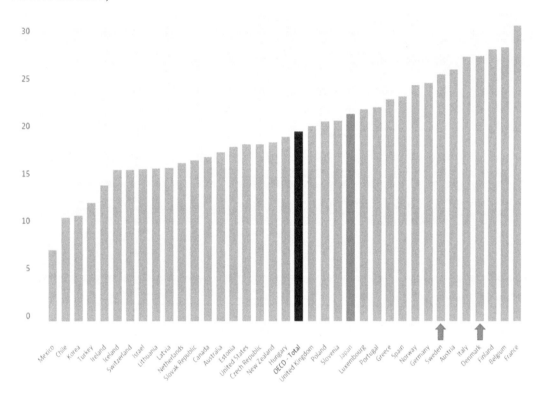

Chart 49 shows public social security expenditures as a percentage of GDP for OECD countries in 2018. The darker bars show those of Japan and the average of OECD countries. Japan is slightly above the OECD average. The aforementioned Denmark and Sweden, which are indicated with arrows, are considerably higher than Japan.

The social security system is a system in which the state or society guarantees income through income transfer and provides social services such as medical care and nursing care in order to prevent poverty, help the poor, and stabilize their lives in the face of life problems such as illness, injury, disability, childbirth, aging, and unemployment, which can be regarded as risks to individual citizens.

From our annual income, income tax, individual resident tax, pension insurance premiums, health insurance premiums, long-term care insurance premiums, and unemployment insurance premiums are deducted. In addition, the consumption tax is also partly used to maintain the social security system. In other words, it is the people who support the public social security system financially.

OECD statistics use various classifications for international comparison and statistical processing, such as adopting the concept of Social Expenditure. In any case, in any country, it is the people who financially support the public social security system, and it is the people as a whole who benefit from it. In other words, the social security system is a system in which citizens support each other.

In December 2020, Then-Prime Minister Suga and Natsuo Yamaguchi, the leader of the Komeito Party, agreed to raise the over-the-counter cost of medical care for people aged 75 and older from 10 percent to 20 percent to those with annual incomes of 2 million yen or more. 75 and older currently pay 10 percent of the over-the-counter cost, while those with annual incomes of 3.83 million yen or more pay 30 percent. The increase will be implemented from October 2022 in order to reduce the burden on the working-age population, as the "baby boomers" will begin to turn 75 or older in 2022.

If the social security system is a system in which citizens support each other, then increasing the burden of medical expenses on people over 75, whose income is not expected to increase in any significant way, will only mean the regression of the social security system. Will this really reduce the burden on the working-age population?

People over 75 have been paying the consumption tax and the social insurance premiums for a long time, and now they will see their expected returns cut because the system is no longer sustainable. If these promises are allowed to go unfulfilled, then social insurance premiums will continue to be raised and the returns cut in order to maintain the system. This is not only a problem for people over 75, but also for the working-age people who support the system now and will receive social security in the future.

In my view, this is just a trick to bully the weak and will do little to maintain the health insurance and social security systems. The root of all evil is a "distorted tax system" that worsens the economy and does not even increase tax revenue. 1988 tax revenue was 50.8 trillion yen, and the average tax revenue for the 31 years from 1989 to 2019, when the consumption tax was added to tax revenue, was 50.7 trillion yen. There is no way the social security system can be maintained without an increase in tax revenue for more than 30 years.

Japan's public social security expenditure according to the OECD, seen in Chart 49, is 21.9% in 2018. The nominal GDP for the same year is 548.1 trillion yen, so multiply by 0.219 and you get 120 trillion yen. This means that the Japanese people contribute 120 trillion yen to the public social security system in some form, including the consumption tax, and receive the same amount of services in some form.

Therefore, in the next section, we will look at the breakdown of social security expenditures and the sources of funding from the Ministry of Finance's website, "Thinking about Japan's Finances."

48. Breakdown of social security expenditures and source of funds

Chart 50: Breakdown of social security expenditures and financial resources (Source: Ministry of Finance)

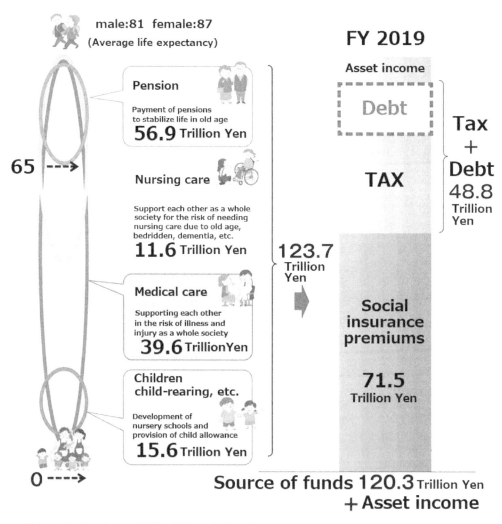

(Note: translated by Arata Yaguchi)

Chart 50 shows the breakdown of social security expenditures and funding sources for FY 2019. The left side shows the breakdown of social security expenditures, and the right side shows the financial resources. The amount is about 120 trillion yen, which is identical to the OECD figure. The breakdown is from the largest amount to the smallest: pensions, medical care, childcare, and nursing care, and the main financial sources are insurance premiums and taxes.

The fact that the insurance premium in the lower right corner is so large, at 71.5 trillion yen, is likely to increase the economic slowdown effect of the consumption tax that we have discussed so far. We can also see that even after collecting such a large amount of premiums and supplementing it with taxes, the government is still in the red and needs to borrow money. This is the situation before the Corona pandemic. This means that unless some measures are taken, the social security system, which is supposed to be a necessity, will become unsustainable in a matter of time.

There is no need to reiterate the importance of the four items in the breakdown, all of which are essential as a safety net for society. In the next section, we will take a look at pensions and health care, the two largest items in terms of the amount of money involved.

49. Dependence of the elderly on pensions

Chart 51: Dependence of the elderly on pensions (Source: Ministry of Health, Labour and Welfare)

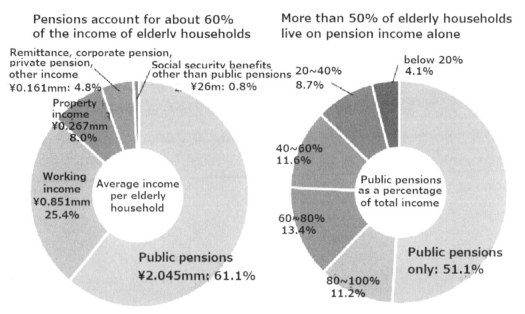

(Source: Ministry of Health, Labour and Welfare, 2018 National Survey on Living Standards)

(Note: translated by Arata Yaguchi)

Chart 51 is from the Ministry of Health, Labour, and Welfare's FY 2019 budget-based scale and role of public pensions. All explanatory notes in the graph are also by the Ministry of Health, Labour and Welfare.

The dependence of the elderly on pensions on the right side shows that 51.1% of households aged 65 and over are living solely on public pension income. In other words, if the pension system cannot be maintained, and even if the system can be maintained, if it cannot provide enough to live on, it is highly unlikely that even social stability can be maintained.

In December 2020, the Suga administration agreed to raise the over-the-counter cost of medical care for those aged 75 and over from 10 percent to 20 percent to those with annual incomes of 2 million yen or more. 75 and over currently pay 10 percent of the bill, while those with annual incomes of 3.83 million yen or more pay 30 percent. The increase will take effect in October 2022.

From the left side of Chart 51, it can be seen that the average pension income of one elderly household is 2,045,000 yen from the public sector alone, and 2,232,000 yen from a combination of remittances, corporate pensions, private pensions and so on. Some young people seem to think that today's elderly are fortunate, but this is the reality of the average. Not only is it not something to envy, but further reductions and increases in medical expenses would be painful, don't you think?

Nevertheless, Japan's economy was growing at a steady pace until FY 1997, and tax revenues were increasing until FY 1990, so when the elderly of today, including myself, were young, we did not feel the pressure that we feel in Japan today. Today, the Japanese economy is in a state of continuous decline in both sales and profits in terms of corporations. And they have been using this as an excuse to worsen employment conditions and reduce benefits. At this rate, it is certain that by the time today's young people become elderly, the average public pension income will be less than half of the current level, in a matter of time.

However, if you young people envy the elderly and reduce the amount of benefits they receive, it will eventually come back to you, and nothing will be solved. It is essential to create a system of the Japanese economy that will increase the revenues and profits. I see in order to do that returning to the pre-1989 tax system would be essential as the first step. Today's senior citizens, including myself, have done nothing for 30 years. Many of them are still preaching the need to raise the consumption tax. The only way to secure your future is for the young people of today to take action yourselves. I hope that this book will be of some help to you.

50. National health insurance

Chart 52: Trends in national health insurance, medical expense and benefits (Source: Compiled from e-Stat data)

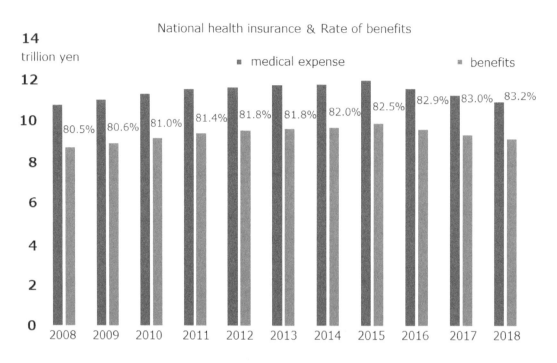

Chart 52 shows the trends in medical expense, medical benefits, and insurance benefit ratios in the National Health Insurance from FY 2008 to FY 2018. The longer bars show the trends in medical expenses, the shorter ones show the trends in medical benefits, and the percentages show the ratio of benefits to medical expenses.

Medical expenses peaked at ¥11.9921 trillion in FY 2015, and benefits will begin to decline accordingly, starting at ¥9.8956 trillion in the same year. On the other hand, the rates of benefits have been consistently increasing.

National Health Insurance, whose insurer is the local government, is for people who are not covered by employer based health insurance or other public medical insurance. The main insured of the National Health Insurance are the self-employed, agricultural workers, and freelancers. Retirees who do not wish to voluntarily continue their employer based health insurance after retiring from their companies are also required to join the National Health Insurance.

For years, there have been calls for medical expense restraint due to the deteriorating balance of payments of the medical insurance system. Looking at Chart 51, one might think that the effect of these medical expense restraints began to emerge around FY 2015, resulting in a decrease in the benefit burden while increasing the benefit rate of the national health insurance system. From this, wouldn't it be assumed that the medical expense per patient is decreasing? So, in the next section, let's see if medical expense per patient are being controlled.

51. Medical expense per capita

Chart 53: Medical expense per person insured by National Health Insurance (Source: Compiled from e-Stat data)

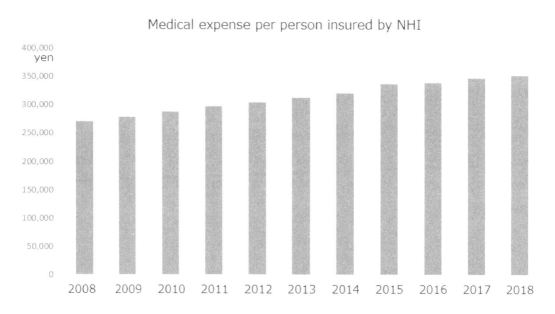

Chart 53 shows the annual medical expenses per insured person from FY 2008 to FY 2018. This shows that the medical expenses per insured person have been rising steadily, reaching 352,917 yen in FY 2018. Of this amount, the National Health Insurance (NHI), shown in the previous Chart 51, pays 293,627 yen (83.2% of the benefit rate), which means that the average patient burden is 59,290 yen per person.

In Japan, in addition to the National Health Insurance, there is a health insurance system for employees and employers of companies. This employer based health insurance is further divided into "union health insurance" and "association health insurance". The union health insurance system is a system in which large companies establish their own health insurance association for their employees, and employees and employers of those companies can join. On the other hand, employees of small and medium-sized companies are generally enrolled in the association health insurance, which is run by the Health Insurance Association of Japan.

On November 5, 2020, the Federation of Health Insurance Associations, a federation of union health insurance run by large corporations and other organizations, announced its revenue and expenditure forecast for the next three years. It is estimated that the time when the insurance premium rate will rise to the level where breakups will occur frequently will be in FY 2021, one year earlier than the previously assumed FY 2022 due to the Corona pandemic.

According to the forecast, the total premium income of about 1,400 union health insurances nationwide will decline from 8.2 trillion yen in FY 2019 to 7.9 trillion yen in FY 2020 and 7.6 trillion yen in FY 2021 and 2022. This is because wages will decline due to worsening corporate performance, and the premiums paid by companies and employees will decrease. On the other hand, medical expenses are expected to increase and the balance of payments will worsen as patients gradually come back after having refrained from seeing a doctor during the pandemic.

In FY 2021, the deficit is expected to be 670 billion yen, and the premium rate needed to break even will be 10.22%, which is above the 10% threshold for a break-up crisis. 10% is the rate charged by the Health Insurance Association of Japan, which undermines the advantage of companies having their own union health insurance.

In fact, a study by the Nihon Keizai Shimbun found that between FY 2009 and FY 2019, about half of union health insurances raised the employee contributions and lowered the corporate portion. In 97% of the unions, the average premium rate rose from 7.37% to 9.22%, and the average premium including the company's portion increased from about 395,000 yen to 526,000 yen.

The Health Insurance Association of Japan, where employees of small and medium-sized companies are joined, is also increasing its contributions, but it is subsidized by the government by more than 1.1 trillion yen a year to avoid a sharp increase in the current 10% premium rate.

What this suggests is that health insurance systems, whether privately or publicly owned, are becoming increasingly difficult to maintain.

The reason why the total medical expense seen in the previous Chart 52 is decreasing, in spite of the medical expense per person in Chart 53 is increasing, is due to a decrease in the number of households and an even greater decrease in the number of insured persons, according to the e-Stat data (see URL at the end of this report). Japan claims to have a universal health insurance system, but this implies that more and more people are falling out of it.

In Chart 51 above, we saw that 51.1% of the households aged 65 and over were living on public pension income alone. And the average income per household of those aged 65 and over was found to be 3,349,000 yen, or 2,045,000 yen if limited to public pensions income alone.

In other words, more than half of all elderly households live on the public pension of 2,045,000 yen, which means that if there is one patient in the household, the remaining household budgets will be 1,986,000 yen, and if there are two, only 1,927,000 yen will remain. In addition, a percentage of the consumption tax is deducted from this amount. This shows that most elderly households are on the edge of not being able to afford any further reduction in their pensions or increase in the burden of the medical insurance system.

52. Government spending on education

Chart 54: International comparison of fiscal expenditure on education (Source: Ministry of Finance)

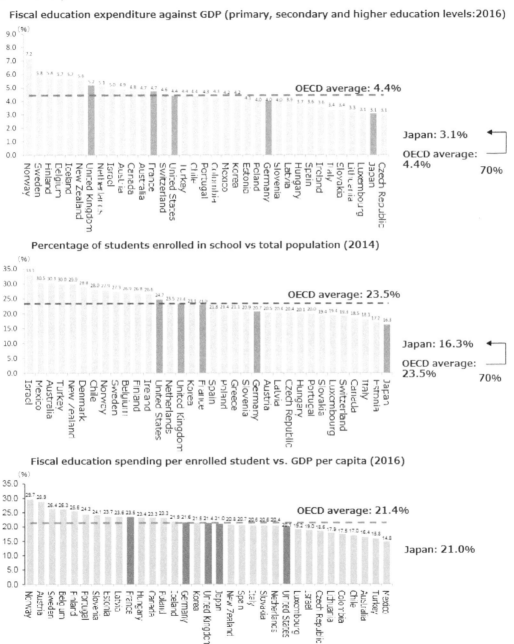

(Note: translated by Arata Yaguchi)

Chart 54 shows an international comparison of fiscal expenditure on education as a percentage of GDP. The bars in the top row show an international comparison of fiscal education expenditure as a percentage of GDP. The middle bars show the number of students enrolled in elementary, middle, and high school as a percentage of the total population. The bars in the bottom row show fiscal expenditure on education per student compared with GDP per capita. Although education expenditure here is not included in the social security system, it is no less important than the above four items, so we will discuss it here.

As seen in the chart in the top row, Japan's education expenditure is the second lowest from the far right, only 70% of the OECD average. Only one country, the Czech Republic, spends less than Japan. Incidentally, the dark bars are for the G5 countries, showing that Japan is far behind.

The chart in the middle shows that Japan's low expenditure on education is due to the small number of pupils in the population. In other words, unless Japan's post-compulsory or high school education rate has declined sharply among OECD countries, it can be suggested that the country has the lowest birthrate and the most aged population.

And the chart at the bottom shows that on a per student basis, Japan's education expenditure is neither high nor low in the OECD average. It is up to you the readers to judge what they think of this, as it is neither good nor bad.

Nevertheless, what we have discussed so far is that the consumption tax hike, which is supposed to be the source of funds for social security spending, has in fact increased social security spending through the economic downturn caused by the tax hike. On the other hand, the economic downturn and income tax cuts have reduced the total tax revenue that is the source of funding. This has been the main cause of the huge accumulated budget deficit and huge public debt. In addition, I have pointed out that the economic downturn may have reduced the competitiveness of companies, worsened the labor environment, and led to the widening gap between the rich and the poor.

In other words, since tax revenues are not growing, the growth of public education expenditure is limited. Since personal income is not increasing, there is a limit to household spending on education. This may have led to a decline in the quality of education, including university education.

53. Trends in social security-related expenditures

Table 04: Trends in social security-related expenditures (Source: Ministry of Health, Labour and Welfare)

Trends in social security-related expenditures in the national budget ¥100mm(%)

C	1980	1985	1990	1995	2000	2005	2010	C	2013	2014	2015	C	2016	2017	2018
1	82,124 (100.0)	95,740 (100.0)	116,154 (100.0)	139,244 (100.0)	167,666 (100.0)	203,808 (100.0)	272,686 (100.0)	1	291,224 (100.0)	305,175 (100.0)	315,297 (100.0)	1	319,738 (100.0)	324,735 (100.0)	329,732 (100.0)
2	9,559 (11.6)	10,816 (11.3)	11,087 (9.5)	10,532 (7.6)	12,306 (7.3)	19,230 (9.4)	203,363 (74.6)	9	218,475 (75.0)	225,557 (73.9)	231,107 (73.3)	11	113,190 (35.4)	114,831 (34.8)	116,853 (35.4)
												12	112,739 (35.3)	115,010 (34.9)	116,079 (35.2)
												13	29,323 (9.2)	30,130 (9.1)	30,953 (9.4)
3	13,698 (16.7)	20,042 (20.9)	24,056 (20.7)	34,728 (24.9)	36,580 (21.8)	16,443 (8.1)	22,388 (8.2)	2	28,614 (9.8)	29,222 (9.6)	29,042 (9.2)	14	20,241 (6.3)	21,149 (6.4)	21,437 (6.5)
4	51,095 (62.2)	56,587 (59.1)	71,953 (61.9)	84,700 (60.8)	109,551 (65.3)	158,638 (77.8)	39,305 (14.4)	3	38,610 (13.3)	44,480 (14.6)	48,591 (15.4)	15	40,080 (12.5)	40,205 (12.2)	40,524 (12.3)
5	3,981 (4.8)	4,621 (4.8)	5,587 (4.8)	6,348 (4.6)	5,434 (3.2)	4,832 (2.4)	4,262 (1.6)	5	3,539 (1.2)	4,093 (1.3)	4,876 (1.5)	5	2,865 (0.9)	3,042 (0.9)	3,514 (1.1)
6	3,791 (4.6)	3,674 (3.8)	3,471 (3.0)	2,936 (2.1)	3,795 (2.3)	4,664 (2.3)	3,367 (1.2)	10	1,986 (0.7)	1,824 (0.6)	1,681 (0.5)	10	1,360 (0.4)	368 (0.1)	373 (0.1)
7	86,416 (7.5)	99,920 (2.6)	120,521 (6.4)	144,766 (2.9)	174,251 (3.9)	208,178 (3.1)	275,561 (9.5)	7	294,316 (10.3)	307,430 (4.5)	299,146 (△3.0)	7	303,110 (1.3)	306,873 (1.2)	311,262 (1.4)
8	307,332 (10.3)	325,854 (△0.0)	353,731 (3.8)	421,417 (3.1)	480,914 (2.6)	472,829 (△0.7)	534,542 (3.3)	8	539,774 (5.3)	564,697 (4.6)	573,555 (1.6)	8	578,286 (0.8)	583,591 (0.9)	588,958 (0.9)

C=Classification 1=Social security related expenditures 2=Welfare expenses 3=Social welfare expenditures
4=Social insurance costs 5=Health and sanitation expenses 6=Unemployment compensation
7=The budget of the Ministry of Health, Labour and Welfare 8=General expenditures
9=Pension medical care insurance benefit costs 10=Employment and worker's compensation
11=Pension benefit costs 12=Medical benefit costs 13=Nursing care benefit costs
14=Fertility promotion expenses 15=Livelihood assistance and other social welfare expenses

(Note: translated by Arata Yaguchi)

Table 04 shows the breakdown of social security-related expenses in the national budget from 1980 to 2018. Figures are 100 million yen. Figures in parentheses show the classification's percentage of total social security expenditures.

From here, we will look at the government-funded social security system and consider whether the consumption tax is necessary or really helpful in maintaining the system, as many politicians, bureaucrats, and successive governments have deemed it to be.

The top row of Table 04 shows Japan's government-funded social security-related expenditures from 1980 to 2018. All the breakdowns in the bottom row are combined here, so the percentage in parentheses is 100%. From this, I created Chart 54 below. As you can see, the figure increases year by year. I wonder how many people feel uncomfortable when they look at this chart? I myself didn't feel much discomfort and thought it was just like that. However, what if I were to say that this would lead to the collapse of Japan's social security system?

Chart 55: Trends in social security-related expenditures (Source: Compiled from Ministry of Health, Labor and Welfare data)

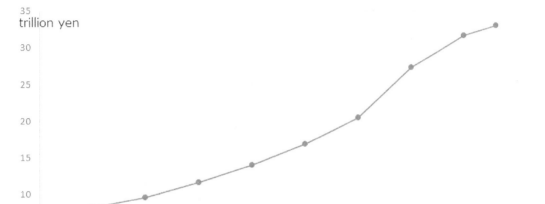

In FY 1990, social security-related expenditures borne by the government were 11.6 trillion yen. This will increase to 33.0 trillion yen in FY 2018. On the other hand, tax revenue was 60.1 trillion yen in FY 1990 and 60.4 trillion yen in FY 2018, which is the double tops of Japan's tax revenue, as I have mentioned. This means that social security-related spending as a percentage of tax revenue has jumped from 19.3% in FY 1990 to 54.6% in FY 2018. You see that more than half of the tax revenue is taken up by social security expenditures paid by the government. Moreover, as we saw in Chart 50 above, it is still not enough, and the government is borrowing money.

And while social security expenditures are expected to continue to rise, tax revenues are expected to decline first due to the consumption tax hike in October 2019, and then more sharply due to the Corona pandemic and the counter-Corona measures. The tax revenue of 60.8 trillion yen in 2020 was owing to the fiscal spending of over 170 trillion yen, and there is no way this can continue.

Covid-19 vaccination has begun worldwide. The Japanese government has spent large sums of money to reserve arrangements for the supply of vaccines from overseas. For example, it has reserved 60 million doses of Pfizer's vaccine, which was announced to be effective in November 2020. Vaccines made by Moderna and AstraZeneca have also been reserved for purchase.

It is fair to say that it is impossible for Japan alone to keep its social security-related expenditures at the level of 30 years ago, while medical costs and drug prices are rising worldwide. The reason why Japan cannot develop its own covid-19 vaccine is because the government does not have the budget to support drug companies. The problem here is that the government is still holding on to the tax revenue from FY 1990 as sort of the largest ever. And it is only since the introduction of the consumption tax that Japan's tax revenue growth has stopped.

Looking at the largest item in the breakdown in Table 04, we can see that social insurance costs which accounted for 60% to nearly 80% of total expenditures until FY 2005 were renamed welfare expenses in FY 2010. From FY 2013 onwards, it was renamed pension medical care insurance benefit costs, and from FY 2016 onwards, it is divided into pension benefit costs, medical benefit costs, and nursing care benefit costs. And if we put those three together, we can see that it has never reached 80% before, but reached 80% in FY 2018.

54. Trends in burden rate of the people

Chart 56: Trends in social security benefit costs (Source: Ministry of Health, Labour and Welfare)

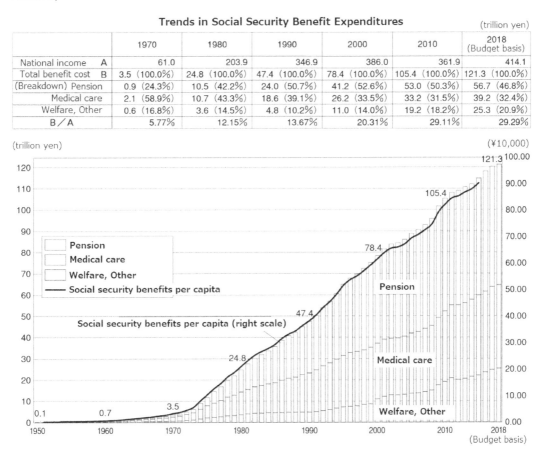

(Note: translated by Arata Yaguchi)

The upper table in Chart 56 shows the trend of social security benefit expenditures for each decade since 1970, the amount of the breakdown and its percentage of the total, and the national burden compared to the national income in percentages. The chart below shows the total cost of social security benefits since 1950, the breakdown of the cost of pensions, medical care, welfare and other on the left scale, and the cost of social security benefits per capita on the right scale. It can be seen that the per capita social security benefit cost reached 900,000 yen in 2015.

First of all, the amount of national income in the top row increased 2.34 times in the first 10 years. This was followed by a 70.1% increase, an 11.3% increase, and a 6.2% decrease. This is in accordance with what we have seen so far: high growth of the economy until the introduction of the consumption tax, a slowdown after the introduction, and negative growth after the tax rate was raised. In the most recent eight years, it has grown by 14.4%, but since it is expected to decline in 2020, it is not expected to reach this figure for the decade.

On the other hand, the cost of benefits has been consistently increasing in all categories, so the public's burden rate has continued to rise from 5.77% to 12.15%, 13.67%, 20.31%, 29.11%, and 29.29%. The rate of increase in the last eight years is slower than the previous two decades, but it is expected to go up more in the decade to 2020.

What these suggest is that in order to maintain the social security system, the burden on the government has increased to 54.6% of total tax revenue as of 2018, as seen in Chart 55, and the burden on the people has continued to increase to 29.3%, as seen in Chart 56. The social security system, which is supposed to be a safety net, has become so heavy that it is threatening to crush both government finances and households. In addition, due to the economic downturn caused by the Corona pandemic and its countermeasures, incomes are expected to decrease and benefit costs are expected to increase, which means that the burden rate of the people is expected to rise much further.

And that will lead to a decline in consumer spending, which will further worsen the economy.

55. Pyramid that became a diamond

Chart 57: Population pyramid (Source: Ministry of Health, Labour and Welfare)

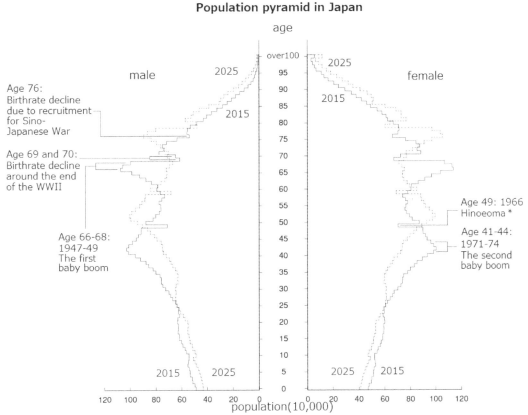

*Note: Hinoeuma. Due to the saying that people born on this year have a very strong personality, birthrates in Japan tend to see a sharp decline.

(Note: translated by Arata Yaguchi)

Chart 57 shows the composition of Japan's population by gender and age. As can be seen in the solid line (2015) and the dashed line (2025), if we move up the population pyramid, we can see that the generation with the widest width, which represents the number of people, will move up. As the lower part of the chart is expected to continue to shrink further, it can no longer be called a pyramid but a diamond. This is the so-called aging society with fewer children.

The increase or decrease in the amount of income and benefits seen in the previous Chart 56 is also affected by the increase or decrease in population. Therefore, examining the data from the Statistics Bureau of the Ministry of Internal Affairs and Communications (URL referenced at the end of this report), the total population of Japan peaked at 128.084 million in 2008, and was estimated to be 125.81 million at the end of September 2020. This is the main reason why both medical costs and benefits of the National Health Insurance have been declining since FY 2015, as seen in Chart 51 above. In other words, if we do not take into account any other conditions, both income and benefits would be expected to decline gradually.

However, it is unrealistic to assume that there are no other conditions.

The declining birthrate is also brought about by a decline in the marriage rate and an increase in the age of marriage. This is partly due to the fact that the growth of the Japanese economy stopped after the introduction of the consumption tax, and the number of young people who want to marry but cannot afford it has increased due to the worsening of employment conditions, such as non-regular employment, and the continued decline in real wages. Another major factor is the lack of budget for creating an environment for working women due to the decrease in tax revenue.

What is predicted by the diamond-shaped population structure is a decrease in the number of workers, an increase in the number of pensioners, and an increase in the medical expenses. This implies a decline in income and an increase in benefits, which will further increase the government's and the people' s burden of social security expenses, which had been rising even before the aging of the population.

However, the advancement of computerization and remote work may encourage both male and female workers to increase their productivity. This is because commuting time will be reduced and the time spent in meetings, which has been considered mostly wasted in the past, can be used for economic activities such as production and consumption.

On the other hand, the deterioration of health due to covid-19 and counter-Coronavirus measures may increase the burden of medical expenses. The health hazards caused by covid-19, which is an epidemic, are obvious, but so are the health hazards caused by its counter-covid-19 measure, nesting. This is because nesting denies all the things that have been considered necessary to maintain good health, such as going out, getting moderate exercise, interacting with people, and engaging in a variety of hobbies. In addition, nesting weight gain due to lack of exercise is believed to increase the risk of serious illness in the event of coronary infection. In addition, stress and sleeplessness due to poor economic conditions have been regarded as major enemies of health.

56. Causes of death among Japanese

Chart 58: Trends in mortality rates by cause of death (Source: Ministry of Health, Labour and Welfare)

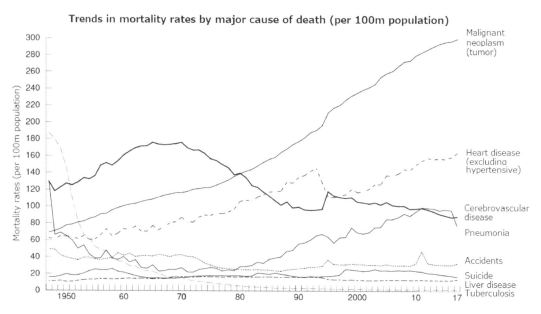

(Note: translated by Arata Yaguchi)

Chart 58 shows the mortality rate by cause of death in Japan after World War II. It can be seen that deaths from tuberculosis, which was the most common cause of death at the time, have decreased dramatically.

A malignant neoplasm is a cancer. The causes of cancer may vary depending on the type of cancer, but stress is also said to be the worst. Cardiovascular and liver diseases could be prevented by adhering to what was believed to be necessary to maintain good health. In addition, we are beginning to see a sharp increase in suicide rates. Suicide has a history of spiking due to stress and insomnia caused by poor economic conditions. In addition, it is believed that people with chronic illnesses may have exacerbated their symptoms as they avoid seeing doctors for fear of Corona infection.

The biggest concern of all may be that viruses and bugs, which seem to be gaining momentum due to global warming, may bring about a series of epidemic pandemics. For more information on this, please read "Plagues and Peoples" by William. H. McNeil. The book describes the history of the battle between plagues and peoples from at the birth of human beings to the end of the 20th century.

All of this strongly suggests that the ever-increasing burden of medical expenses is unlikely to start decreasing. In other words, it is clear that it will be difficult to maintain the social security system without securing some reliable kind of financial resources.

57. Estimate of Ministry of Health, Labour and Welfare

Chart 59: Review of social security benefits and burdens (Source: Ministry of Health, Labour and Welfare)

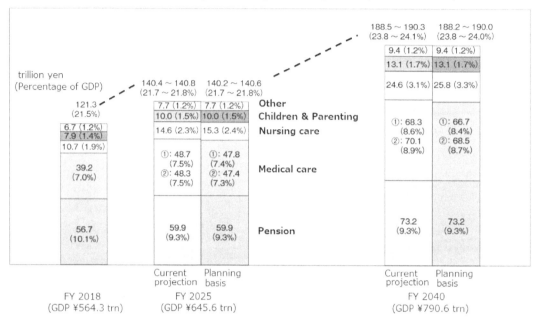

(Note: translated by Arata Yaguchi)

Chart 59 shows a review of social security benefits and burdens by the Ministry of Health, Labour and Welfare, but after just one glance at the chart, I lost interest in looking at the figures in detail. This is because the future GDP forecast is a pipe dream that deviates greatly from past actual figures.

It is out of the question to assume that the size of the economy will increase to 645.6 trillion yen in 7 years and to 790.6 trillion yen in 22 years. This means that the economy is expected to grow by 14.4% in 7 years and by 40.1% in 22 years. Is the fact that the later 15 years are more decelerating a reflection of the declining birthrate and aging population?

In any case, these figures suggest that the consumption tax revenue, which is expected to stabilize at slightly more than 20 trillion yen, cannot be a source of funding for the ever-increasing social security expenditures.

In FY 1990, when total tax revenue was virtually the highest, income tax revenue was 26 trillion yen and corporate tax revenue was 18.4 trillion yen, for a total of 44.4 trillion yen. The nominal GDP at that time was 456 trillion yen. On the other hand, nominal GDP in FY 2018 was 548.1 trillion yen, which was the largest year on record for both corporate sales and corporate profits. This means that if tax rates were the same, income tax revenue and corporate tax revenue in FY 2018 should have been expected to be quite large. In reality, however, income tax revenue was 19.9 trillion yen and corporate tax revenue was 12.3 trillion yen, for a total of 32.2 trillion yen. While the size of the economy has increased by 20.2%, tax revenue has decreased by 27.5%. This makes it nearly impossible to avoid the deficit.

Expenditures for FY 2020 were 175.7 trillion yen, while tax revenues were announced to be 60.8 trillion yen. With the largest source of revenue here being the consumption tax, which is stable at slightly more than 20 trillion yen, Japan's finances will go bankrupt. If the social security system does not go bankrupt in such an environment, it is to continue the system only in form to protect the employment of the organizations and to reduce the benefits to a mere pittance.

Let's call up Chart 04 again and take a look at it. This is the reality of the Japanese economy. 20 years ago, Japan's population was still growing, the accumulated deficit and public debt were much smaller than now, and the competitiveness of companies as well as education level were far better than now. Nevertheless, Japan's economy has been stagnant for more than 20 years, despite making the monetary easing to the limit.

To emphasize the point, with the economy is aging at one of the fastest rates in the world with a declining birthrate, the world's largest accumulated deficit and outstanding public debt relative to the size of the economy, the competitiveness of companies and the level of education have dropped significantly, and the economy is burdened with a monetary policy that cannot be eased any further, Japan's economic scale of 500 trillion yen is expected to increase to 645.6 trillion yen in the next seven years and 790.6 trillion yen in 22 years. This is the estimate of the authority in charge. It is a nightmare for the people, isn't it?

Chart 04: Trends in nominal GDP and growth rate and consumption tax rate (Source: Compiled from data of the Cabinet Office)

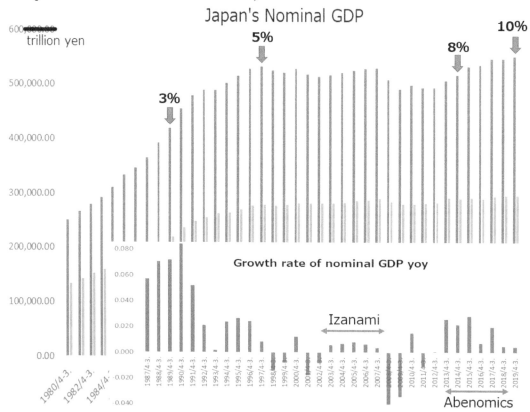

A possible achievement of this assumption would be to return to the growth curve before the 3% arrow in Chart 04 above. This means revitalizing the economy by eliminating the consumption tax, and at the same time, promoting progressive income taxation and raising the corporate tax rate in order to secure tax revenue.

Afterword: From decline to prosperity

After reading this book, has your perception of the current state of the Japanese economy changed? Do you share the same sense of crisis with me about Japan's finances and social security system?

A recession hurts households by reducing income and the national treasury by reducing tax revenues. This means that the ability of households and the national treasury to support social security will decrease, at the time when the need for social security increases and social security expenditures rise. And the increased burden of such social insurance premiums will lead to a death spiral of decreasing disposable income and further economic recession. This implies that economic growth is to be of paramount importance.

What I have learned from my own analysis of the 65 charts and tables in this book is that Japan's push for deregulation since the 1990s to open up the country to foreign countries has not helped the country's economic growth or the welfare of its citizens. In addition, Japan's high consumption tax and social insurance premiums have put pressure on consumer spending, which is likely contributing to the economic recession.

However, the social security system is on the edge, and social insurance premiums cannot be lowered. In this respect, Japan is cornered.

However, there is no need for you the readers to be overly pessimistic about the future of Japan. Because the future can be changed. We don't need to look at long history. How many things have changed in the past decade alone?

Just like the introduction of the consumption tax in 1989 and the increase in the tax rate to 5% in 1997, which almost instantly changed the trend of Japan's economy from prosperity to decline, eliminating the consumption tax could change the trend from decline to prosperity in a matter of years.

Tax revenue in FY 1988 was 50.8 trillion yen, and the average tax revenue for the 31 years from FY 1989 to FY 2019, when the consumption tax was added to tax revenue, was 50.7 trillion yen. In light of the fact that Japan's economy grew 1.41 times (in yen) and the world's grew 4.42 times (in dollars) during this period, it is hard to find such an obvious cause for decline. If only this distorted tax system could be changed, there is a good chance that Japan would improve. If Japan were to grow at the same rate as the rest of the world, and if tax revenues were to increase as they did under the tax system in those days, tax revenues for fiscal 2019 would have reached 224.5 trillion yen.

Let me give you a few reasons why I think the trend could be changed from decline to prosperity, if proper measures are taken.

1. Japan's economy is still the third largest in the world
2. Net financial assets of households was 1553 trillion yen as of the end of September 2020.
3. Net financial assets of private non-financial corporations was 243 trillion yen as of the end of September 2020.
4. Japan's net overseas assets was 386 trillion yen as of the end of September 2020.
5. The loan-deposit gap of 109 domestic banks was 319 trillion yen as of the end of September 2020.
6. Pension assets (GPIF) was 173 trillion yen as of the end of September 2020
7. A universal health insurance system has been established.

These are some of the most highly valued in the world. In addition, the country has what it takes to lead the world in areas such as science and technology, culture, sports, and subcultures.

In addition to investing in stocks and corporate bonds, a growing number of banks are using ESG assessments as a reference in their lending. The ESG investment is something that major institutional investors around the world are making a shift towards.

In this context, in October 2020 the Wall Street Journal published a list of the top sustainably managed companies, taking a broad view of sustainability, assessing a company's leadership and governance practices for their ability to create value for shareholders over the long term. The ranking was produced by the Journal's environment, social and governance research analysts, who assessed more than 5,500 publicly traded businesses based on a range of sustainability metrics.

And sixteen Japanese companies were selected in the top 100, with Sony in first place.

No. 1, Sony
No. 10, Sekisui Chemical
No. 13, AGC
No. 36, Canon Inc.
No. 38, Brother Industries, Ltd.
No. 44, Omron
No. 46, Kyocera Corporation
No. 56, Ushio Inc.
No. 57, JFE
No. 59, Konica Minolta
No. 66, Ebara Corporation
No. 77, TOTO
No. 79, Hitachi Ltd.
No. 82, Obayashi Corporation
No. 87, Toshiba Corporation
No. 97, Fujikura Ltd.

Reference: Explore the Full WSJ Sustainable Management Ranking
https://www.wsj.com/articles/explore-the-full-wsj-sustainable-management-ranking-11602506733

Even though this is just one way of evaluating it, it is still number one out of

5,500 listed companies in the world. And we have 16 companies in the top 100. Japanese companies have not yet been abandoned. Don't you think so? All of this shows that Japan still has a lot of power. It's not too late.

The relentlessly declining birthrate and aging population is a common problem in the developed countries of the world. Most of the world's countries have experienced a sharp increase in unemployment and ballooning budget deficits and public debts as a result of the Corona pandemic, or rather, the countermeasures to it. In addition, a series of abnormal weather events due to global warming, and epidemics that are expected to continue in the future, are common throughout the world. The gap between the rich and the poor has widened worldwide. Despite the ban on gatherings as a measure against covid-19, there have been civil uprisings all over the world. All of this suggests that global security will deteriorate and geopolitical risks will increase.

Japan must confront these problems as the country with the weakest finances in the world. There may not be much time left before these problems lead to a major tragedy. Risk management is urgently needed.

There is not much to lose by eliminating the consumption tax. Historical data strongly suggests that the economy will expand and tax revenues will increase. What Japan needs now is to return to the tax system as it was until FY 1989. This would protect pensions, health care, and education, and give the Japanese people, businesses, and government the possibility of being happier than they are now. If Japan becomes stronger, our allies will also be happy. It could be surprisingly easy to change trends if you know where to look.

This is the kind of information I can offer you to the readers to make a decision. Just like in the market, it is up to you to decide for yourself whether to sell or buy.

Spring, 2021

Arata Yaguchi

References

Ministry of Finance: Fiscal Considerations for the Future of Japan (Japanese)
https://www.mof.go.jp/budget/fiscal_condition/related_data/202007_kanryaku.pdf

Ministry of Finance: Japanese Public Finance Fact Sheet
https://www.mof.go.jp/english/budget/budget/fy2020/04.pdf

Cabinet Office: National Accounts (GDP Statistics)
https://www.esri.cao.go.jp/jp/sna/menu.html

Ministry of Finance: Accounting Information and PDCA Cycle
https://www.mof.go.jp/budget/fiscal_condition/related_data/202007_05.pdf

United Nations Statistics Division: National Accounts - Analysis of Main Aggregates
https://unstats.un.org/unsd/snaama/Index

Statistics Bureau, Ministry of Internal Affairs and Communications: Labor Force Survey Long-Term Time Series Data
https://www.stat.go.jp/data/roudou/longtime/03roudou.html#hyo_1

National Confederation of Trade Unions: International Comparison of Real Wage Indexes
https://www.zenroren.gr.jp/jp/housei/data/2018/180221_02.pdf

Ministry of Health, Labour and Welfare: Social security-related materials
https://www.mhlw.go.jp/wp/hakusyo/kousei/18-2/dl/01.pdf

Bank of Japan:
https://www.boj.or.jp/

Ministry of Finance: Interest Rate Information
https://www.mof.go.jp/jgbs/reference/index.html

Ministry of Finance: Necessity and Efforts for Fiscal Consolidation
https://www.mof.go.jp/budget/fiscal_condition/related_data/202007_02.pdf

e-Stat: Consumer Price Index
https://dashboard.e-stat.go.jp/timeSeriesResult?indicatorCode=0703010401010090000

Ministry of Finance: Part 1: Japanese Government Finances
https://www.mof.go.jp/budget/fiscal_condition/related_data/202007_01.pdf

National Tax Agency: Corporate Tax Rate
https://www.nta.go.jp/taxes/shiraberu/taxanswer/hojin/5759.htm

National Tax Agency: Company sample survey (loss-making corporations)
https://www.nta.go.jp/publication/statistics/kokuzeicho/kaishahyohon2018/pdf/h30.pdf

National Tax Agency: Income Tax Rates
https://www.nta.go.jp/taxes/shiraberu/taxanswer/shotoku/2260.htm

Ministry of Finance: Income Tax Rate Structure
https://www.mof.go.jp/tax_policy/summary/income/b02.htm

Ministry of Finance: Materials on consumption tax, etc. (consumption taxation)
https://www.mof.go.jp/tax_policy/summary/itn_comparison/j04.htm

Ministry of Finance: Income Tax Rates in Major Countries
https://www.mof.go.jp/tax_policy/summary/income/234.pdf

OECD： General government debt
https://data.oecd.org/gga/general-government-debt.htm#indicator-chart

Ministry of Finance: Japan's Financial Data (July 2020)
https://www.mof.go.jp/budget/fiscal_condition/related_data/202007.html

International Monetary Fund: Fiscal Policy in a Post-Corona World
https://www.imf.org/ja/News/Articles/2020/07/10/blog-fiscal-policies-for-a-transformed-world

OECD： Revenue Statistics 2019
http://www.oecd.org/tax/revenue-statistics-2522770x.htm

Ministry of Foreign Affairs of Japan: Basic Data on the Kingdom of Denmark
https://www.mofa.go.jp/mofaj/area/denmark/data.html#section4

Facebook: Embassy of Denmark
https://www.facebook.com/EmbassyDenmark/posts/1241264725910048/

Ministry of Foreign Affairs of Japan: Basic Data on the Kingdom of Sweden
https://www.mofa.go.jp/mofaj/area/sweden/data.html#section1

OECD： Corporate Tax Statistics
https://www.oecd.org/tax/tax-policy/corporate-tax-statistics-second-edition.pdf

Tax Foundation： Global Corporate Tax Rates (2019)
https://taxfoundation.org/publications/corporate-tax-rates-around-the-world/

OECD： General government deficit
https://data.oecd.org/gga/general-government-deficit.htm

OECD： Social spending
https://data.oecd.org/socialexp/social-spending.htm

Ministry of Finance: What is the Growing Social Security?
https://www.mof.go.jp/zaisei/aging-society/society-security.html

Ministry of Health, Labour and Welfare: Size and Role of Public Pensions
https://www.mhlw.go.jp/content/000574084.pdf

e-Stat: Monthly report of national health insurance industry
https://www.e-stat.go.jp/

Ministry of Health, Labour and Welfare: Social security-related materials
https://www.mhlw.go.jp/wp/hakusyo/kousei/18-2/dl/01.pdf

Statistics Bureau, Ministry of Internal Affairs and Communications: Population estimates
https://www.stat.go.jp/data/jinsui/new.html

Bank of Japan: Flow of Funds in the Third Quarter of 2020
https://www.boj.or.jp/statistics/sj/sjexp.pdf

About the author: Arata Yaguchi

Born in 1954. Waseda University (incomplete). The University of Melbourne (BA). Worked as a foreign exchange and bond dealer and institutional sales at Nomura Securities, Solomon Brothers, and Union Bank of Switzerland (UBS) and so on.

Currently, CEO of TPA Inc. and a lecturer at "Investment School Premium" run by Financial Intelligence Inc.

Books: "Survival Dealing", "Arata Yaguchi's Short-Term Trading Class", "Swing Trading with Limited Risk" and more than a dozen.

Reference: http://aratayaguchi.web.fc2.com/

Reference : Quiz Book

What has made Japan's economy stagnant for more than 30 years?
57 questions to reveal the problems of the Japanese economy
(Arata Yaguchi: Kindle Edition)
https://www.amazon.com/dp/B09K5M8895/

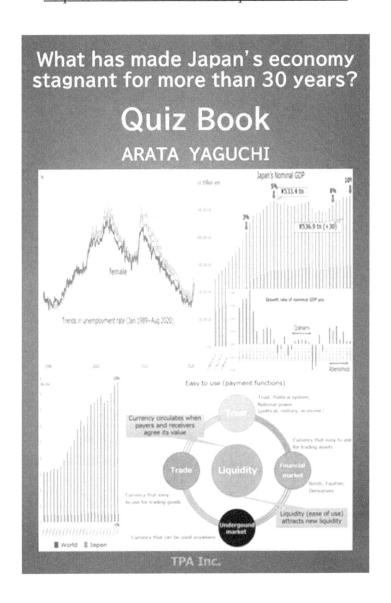

Reference: Original Japanese Version

The System that makes Japan happy
How to protect the pension and health care systems
(Arata Yaguchi: Kindle Edition)
https://www.amazon.co.jp/dp/B092W1M8MZ/

Reference: Original Japanese Version

Quiz Book: The System that makes Japan happy
57 Questions to Reveal the Problems of the Japanese Economy
(Arata Yaguchi: Kindle Edition)
https://www.amazon.co.jp/dp/B09HV3B8YC/

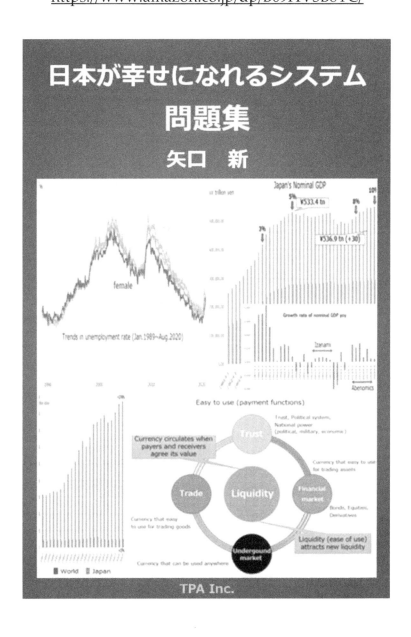

Printed in France by Amazon
Brétigny-sur-Orge, FR

11054057R00118